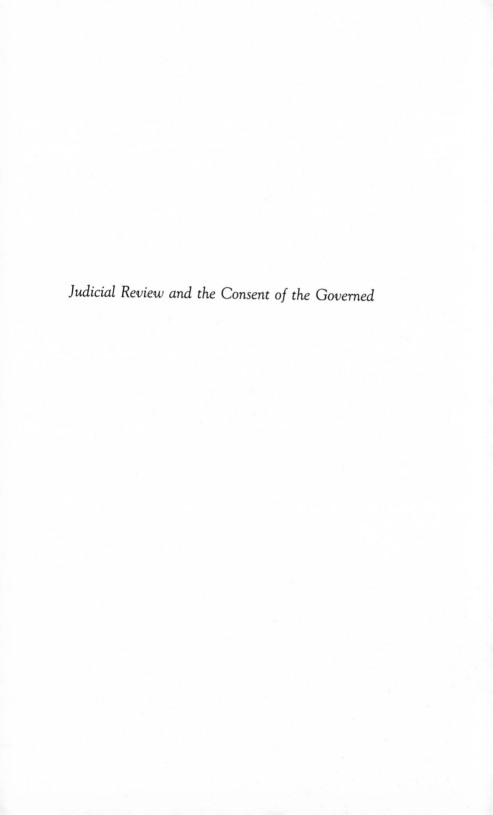

*Judicial Review and the Consent of the Governed*

# Judicial Review and the Consent of the Governed

## Activist Ways and Popular Ends

*by*

Donald E. Lively

McFarland & Company, Inc., Publishers
*Jefferson, North Carolina, and London*

British Library Cataloguing-in-Publication data are available


Library of Congress Cataloguing-in-Publication Data

Lively, Donald E., 1947–
    Judicial review and the consent of the governed : activist ways
and popular ends / Donald E. Lively.
       p.   cm.
    Includes bibliographical references and index.  ∞
    ISBN 0-89950-524-4 (lib. bdg. : 55# alk. paper)
    1. Judicial review–United States–History.  2. Political
questions and judicial power–United States–History.  I. Title.
KF4575.L48   1990
347.73'12–dc20
[347.30712]                                            89-43699
                                                           CIP

Manufactured in the United States of America

McFarland & Company, Inc., Publishers
  Box 611, Jefferson, North Carolina 28640

To Mom and Dad
who made everything possible
and
my wife Pam, and Rico
who make everything wonderful.

# Acknowledgments

Several persons have played essential roles in the preparation of this book. In particular, Fran Molnar was responsible for most of the word processing and with consistent good spirit accepted the risk that my writing presented to her eyesight. The staff of City University of Hong Kong graciously typed the original draft during the course of my visit there as a senior lecturer. Derek Roebuck, head of the Department of Law at CUHK, provided support and guidance in the book's formative stages. I benefited too from my year as a clerk to the Honorable Jim R. Carrigan who, as a federal judge in Denver, demonstrated many of the virtues of judicial activism and few of its flaws. Finally, I am indebted to my colleagues at the University of Toledo College of Law, who have created an atmosphere remarkably free of the pretensions of academia but nonetheless graced by persons of eminence and excellence in their respective fields.

THE AUTHOR

# Table of Contents

# Introduction

Debate over the role of the judiciary in a democratic society is deep, unending and often self-serving. From the republic's inception, theories of judicial review have abounded and competed. A search for what the founders intended the judiciary's function to be is largely unavailing, since little evidence exists that they contemplated many relevant specifics of the task. Even if they had reflected on the details, it is unlikely that any collective intent could be identified that would cast the judicial function into precise and uncontroverted terms. As debate within the Supreme Court itself revealed within a few years of the constitution's ratification, a cleavage of thought already existed with respect to the values the judiciary could employ as reference points in fashioning legal principle.

Judicial review, which gives the Court final word in declaring what the constitution means and thereby enables it to displace conflicting views and actions of the legislative and executive branches and the states, is a power essentially seized by Chief Justice Marshall in *Marbury v. Madison*. Although the issue may have been controverted at the time, and was shaped by the political agenda of Federalists striving to curb the rising influence of Jeffersonian Republicans, the precept has evolved into an enduring principle of governance. Establishment of the power of judicial review, however, has not resolved the conflict that continues to be perceived between authority exercised by an unelected branch of government and general democratic expectations.

1

Such tension arose even before Marshall arrogated and consolidated judicial power, as evidenced by the dialogue between justices Chase and Iredell regarding the propriety of judicial reference to or invocation of natural law. Even today, much of the discourse is essentially an extension of that debate. Earlier this century, Judge Hand and Justice Black warned against judicial efforts to infuse substantive meaning into the liberty provision of the Fourteenth Amendment. For them and many others, introduction of the right of privacy, economic freedom or any other liberty not specifically enumerated by the constitution itself, no matter how elegantly or circumscriptively stated, represents the operation of natural justice and absence of any limiting principles. Thus, they have railed against the dangers of rule by a "bevy of Platonic Guardians" whose governance would be subjective and antidemocratic. Consistent with or responsive to such concerns, theories of review including literalism, originalism, neutral principles and other process restrictive notions, have multiplied as purported methodologies for ensuring judicial restraint.

Given the fundamental materiality of the subject and absence of any baseline criteria for defining the judiciary's function or testing relevant hypotheses, it is not surprising that the field has proved fertile for academic exercise and competition. Nor is it unexpected that much of what grows there is little more than exotic grist for the mills of academia. Extensive scholarly energy has been devoted, for instance, to considering whether the judiciary in activating open-ended constitutional terms must tie its enunciations to specific explications or clear implications of the charter.

Although conducted on what appears to be a high intellectual plane, much of the discourse misses some fundamental realities that undermine its utility. The constitution has not been retrieved from some archaeological recess. Unlike an ancient scripture, therefore, its meaning is not to be deciphered. Nor is it to be discerned by pondering the document until some revelation occurs. Rather, the constitution speaks in a relative few sweeping principles which acquire practical relevance only when external values are brought to bear upon them. Since selection and importation of those values are essentially subjective processes, constitutional law invariably is a function of the judiciary's extrapolation of societal history, concerns and priorities rather than ordination or inevitability of the document itself.

What is particularly odd about the proliferation of theories favoring restraint and expressions of concern regarding the institution's antidemocratic nature is that the judiciary generally has demonstrated extreme sensitivity toward majoritarian preferences and ways. The tone of much contemporary rhetoric suggests a Court that has run amok in subjectivism. Characterizations akin to those branding the Warren Court as wildly activist, for expanding civil rights and liberties, constructing new freedoms and advancing rights of the accused, are being trotted out anew in response to the Rehnquist Court's hostility toward affirmative action, lack of sensitivity to the realities of racism and movement to narrow a woman's liberty to obtain an abortion. Such depictions are exaggerated, however, and not supported by a broad view of reality.

The Court historically has been mostly reluctant to activate the constitution in a fashion that invites popular disapproval. The Ninth and Fourteenth amendments, for instance, provide the Court with unlimited opportunities for subjectivism. It has responded by refusing even the mildest effort to define, pursuant to the Ninth Amendment, rights not enumerated by the constitution and "retained by the people." By consistently declining the Ninth Amendment's own invitation to make substantive sense of it, the Court has evinced a circumspection that effectively freezes the provision but is consistent with a general inclination toward restraint rather than adventure.

The same tendency is visible in the history of the liberty and equal protection components of the Fourteenth Amendment. Judicial response to vitalizing those guarantees has been spotty and even scornful. The equal protection clause for most of its history has countenanced the separate but equal doctrine (or merely the separate). Until the middle part of this century, the equal protection guarantee was largely disdained by the Court. Even what arguably may be the judiciary's most assertive contemporary pronouncement—

declaring official segregation, unlawful—eventually was confined geographically and defined conceptually in accordance with majoritarian preferences.

Reality when examined dispassionately shows that popular sentiment almost invariably prevails in determining constitutional perimeters because the Court usually is sensitive to it or, in the event of miscalculation, becomes attuned to and ultimately responds to it. For a variety of reasons, detailed later, the judiciary is subject to significant democratic influences and, as a consequence, is decidedly majoritarian and seldom a threat to democratic principles or expectations. Neither the elected branches of government nor the public would countenance a different reality.

The possibility that the Court may be subjective in a way that overrides popular instinct or rationality has been a source of much political fodder. Its value, however, has been more rhetorical than substantive. Richard Nixon's promise to appoint strict constructionists to the Court, for instance, translated into a mere alteration of subjective priorities. Strict constructionism proved to be a code for narrowing the rights of the accused, curbing expansion of the desegregation mandate beyond the South, and terminating busing to achieve racial balance in schools. It did not preclude the Court from expanding the right of privacy to include the liberty to elect an abortion, nor delimit the freedom later.

Recognition of the right to elect an abortion itself has been identified and denounced as a leading example of law created by the Court rather than by the constitution. Because most constitutional law of significance is crafted by the Court, the characterization may be sound but the criticism is not. Relentless legislative challenges to the Court created right and continuing judicial review and recalibration of its contours reflect the abiding pertinence of rather than dismissal of popular preference. It is neither unusual nor should it be disturbing for the judiciary to be subjective. What would be extraordinary is if it were subjective in a way that departed from or failed eventually to factor in conventional sentiment.

A central premise of this book is that activism, subjectively referenced to extraconstitutional values, reflects a legitimate function

4

of the judiciary. Although some constitutional passages akin to those setting the age for holding elective office lend themselves to precise understanding, the delineation of enumerated and unenumerated rights requires importation of values and engraftment of principles upon the constitution. What results from that process, since close-ended terms and provisions are never litigated, is the bulk of constitutional law. Several instances, including the Court's prolonged emphasis upon economic liberty during the first third of this century, might be adverted to as evidence that the judiciary is capable of disregarding popular sentiment and adopting a dangerously antidemocratic position. Such review has proved to be the exception rather than the rule and, even as an abuse, eventually demonstrated the limitations of judicial power and unabating tug of democratic influence. Given a record that consistently reveals an inclination toward majoritarian ways, a more trenchant concern may be with hypersensitivity toward those conventions.

# One
# Myths and Realities
# of Judicial Review

A common refrain about American government is that it is a system "of laws and not of men."[1] The characterization is handy albeit rough terminology for distinguishing a society committed to principles of consistency and fair play rather than one subject to the whims of authoritarian rule. Like many convenient phrases that attempt neatly to capture a complex point, however, it oversimplifies and if taken too literally misleads. The dictum traces back to one of the Supreme Court's earliest but most enduring opinions. The case of *Marbury v. Madison*[2] itself examined not a sterile body of law but one mixed with ideology, partisanship and personality.[3] Implicit in the substance if not rhetoric of the decision is that a formal political system, requiring conception, comprehension, administration and enforcement of legal principle, can divorce neither law nor men from the other.

Law, such as that concerning the thermodynamics of gravity, requires no human construction or oversight to effectuate its governance of the physical world. Principles which describe and predict natural realities, however, are of a different class than law which prescribes standards for human behavior. Positive law, which governs the institutions and citizenry of organized society, requires creativity rather than mere acknowledgment and is evolutionary instead of immutable. Some human-made law is so clear in its meaning and aim that effectuation merely requires articulation,

7

monitoring and enforcement of its demands. A law requiring motorists to stop at a red light, for instance, imposes an obligation that is manifest and sets a standard by which compliance or breach is readily discerned.

Much societal law, however, is neither self-executing nor self-evident. That dual reality is nowhere more apparent than in the progress, twists and gyrations of the nation's most fundamental governing principles. The American constitution is replete with provisions and guarantees that are more open-ended than precise. Some of its terms even now have been largely unexamined or undeveloped,[4] while others have a tortuous record that continues to unfold.

The constitution, for instance, has guaranteed equal protection for more than a century.[5] Neither the ultimate meaning nor effectuation of the principle was secured, however, by its ratification as part of the Fourteenth Amendment. For most of its history in fact, equal protection has not been taken seriously as a constitutional command. Justice Oliver Wendell Holmes dismissed it little more than half a century ago as "the usual last resort of constitutional arguments."[6] It was the process of human interpretation rather than ordained meaning which begot the separate but equal doctrine as a constitutional premise for legal discrimination.[7] Subsequent generations redefined the Fourteenth Amendment so that it later mandated desegregation,[8] then permitted affirmative action[9] and eventually insisted upon color-blindness regardless of whether a policy was burdensome or remedial in design.[10] The evolution, if not convolution, of such law demonstrates that persons have a central role not only in its creation but in its development. It also denotes a system of governance that more accurately might be identified as one "of law and of men."

The reality, even if it scrambles an otherwise neat slogan, should be neither disturbing nor controversial. A common strategy of modern politics, however, is to arouse and pander to fears associated with the presence of an institution responsible for vitalizing the law. While the process of legislating is accepted as the essence of a representative system, the role of an unelected judiciary in reviewing, and sometimes invalidating popular law may be regarded as discomforting at best and antidemocratic at worst.[11] President Roosevelt played upon those sentiments when, during the Great Depression of the 1930s, the Court consistently invalidated his New Deal policies.[12] In a radio address, Roosevelt declared that:

> we have . . . reached a point as a Nation where we must take action to save the Constitution from the Court and the Court from itself. We must find a way to take an appeal from the Supreme Court to the Constitution itself. We want a Supreme Court which will do justice under the Constitution—not over it.[13]

A few decades later, Richard Nixon responded to the Warren Court's exposition of personal liberties and formulation of aggressive school desegregation remedies by promising, if elected president, to appoint "strict constructionists" to the Supreme Court.[14] A similar appeal to popular anxieties characterized President Bush's campaign pledge to "appoint judges who will interpret the constitution as it is written."[15] Periodic congressional initiatives to strip the Court of jurisdiction to resolve highly charged issues, such as busing for desegregation purposes or school prayer, likewise capitalize upon apprehensions toward the judiciary.[16]

Many allegations of judicial activism tend to be confusing, if not deceiving, partly because the relevant terminology is seldom defined. Activism wears a variety of faces that may range from displacing legislative action to refusing to hear a case. The setting aside of state action, because it conflicts with an express constitutional provision, is unmistakably interventionist. Controversy would be unlikely, however, if the Court declared the election of more then two senators from a state to be unconstitutional. Such activism would generate little if any debate, because the Court merely would be effectuating explicit and undisputable constitutional terms.[17]

Activism is more likely to bestir controversy when the judiciary attempts to inject meaning into text that is not self-defining. The constitution, for instance, empowers Congress "to regulate Commerce . . . among the Several States"[18] but provides no definition of what constitutes interstate commerce. How the Court fills that

9

textual void is critical to the scope of congressional authority. Narrow construction of the commerce clause earlier this century precluded federal regulation of conditions in the workplace, while contemporary interpretations are so broad that the commerce power is a source not only of employment but civil rights, criminal and environmental law.[19] The need for a judicial role in supplying constitutional meaning when it is not clear from the text itself is undeniable. The Bill of Rights, which may be cast in absolute or generalized terms, requires definition, adaptation and sometimes reconciliation of internal tension. Line-drawing is resorted to, for instance, in determining what type of expression is constitutionally protected,[20] when the right to counsel[21] or against excessive bail[22] operates, what constitutes an unreasonable search and seizure or cruel and unusual punishment[23] and so on. The process even may be simultaneously congruent with and at cross-purposes with constitutional principle, as happens when the Court considers laws which would accommodate the free exercise of religion[24] but advance it in violation of the establishment clause.[25]

The setting of any constitutional perimeters is a treacherous exercise insofar as it affords opportunities for standards that are subjective rather than principled. Concern with those perils is especially prominent when the Fourteenth Amendment is implicated. Among other things, the Fourteenth Amendment provides that no "state [shall] deprive any person of life, liberty or property, without Due Process of Law; nor deny to any person . . . equal protection of the laws."[26] It is unlikely that the judiciary functions on grounds more vulnerable to criticism than when it infuses substantive meaning into the Fourteenth Amendment.

Reference to the due process clause as a source for the right of privacy, and to the equal protection clause as the basis for assertive remediation of racial injustice, has engendered some of the loudest protests against contemporary jurisprudence. Typical criticism of decisions recognizing those interests, or expanding them respectively to include the freedom to elect an abortion or insist upon busing to effectuate desegregation, is that the judiciary is cutting law from its own cloth with only token advertence to the constitution.

Such objection perpetuates a controversy which is nearly as old as the republic itself but too often devolves into a fruitless discourse over permissible sources for decision-making. Academic debates over proper reference materials overlook the reality that most any concept of right or freedom can be introduced with an arguable tie to a constitution grounded in unexplicated notions of liberty, equal protection and privileges and immunities.

Judicial activism that enunciates principles tied to extraconstitutional values is an invariable target of opprobrium. Criticism seldom can be taken at face value, however, because it so often enshrouds hypocrisy. Many an appellate judge professing to abide by principles of restraint, and critical of expansive constitutional renderings, at least privately will acknowledge that he or she has disregarded an error at trial because "the defendant probably was guilty anyway." It is even a source of pride with some trial judges that they have relied upon their intuitive rather than deductive senses in finding a defendant guilty.[27] Reliance upon hunches and its consequence, the elevation of personal preference over legal principle, are dubious sources of bragging rights for anyone purporting to advocate judicial restraint. Hunches may be mixed with or interchangeable with racist or other stereotypes which have accounted for much of the nation's unhappy jurisprudential legacy. Their usage may be especially objectionable to the extent they reflect a conscious disregard of established or defined standards for weighing evidence. Such activism categorically is more objectionable than engraftment of constitutional principle, since it is akin to mindful circumvention of a textual mandate. Its operation nonetheless supports observations that restraint is honored more in the breach than in the observance.[28]

Externally referenced activism may be properly denounced insofar as it consists of the use of judicial power merely to advance personal ideology with indifference to whether it contemporaneously or eventually would be acclaimed by the citizenry. It was precisely such ways that accounted for the objectionable jurisprudence which, for the first third of this century, blunted social reform and progress.[29] Unless a conscientious effort is made to explain why a

11

principle unexplicated by the constitution is compelling and flows from values that can be widely subscribed to, judicial creations of law are destined to be considered unprincipled. The likelihood of such consideration is enhanced whenever judges are appointed for ideological purposes.

Although the Reagan Administration publicly decried the evils of activism, it was second to none in its commitment to ideological screening of prospective jurists. While promising judges with a demonstrated "commitment to judicial restraint," Reagan campaigned for the presidency on platforms that explicitly urged appointment of individuals who would "respect traditional family values and the sanctity of human life."[30] The Administration's nomination of judges and justices committed to a particular political and social agenda revealed a selective investment in the judicial ways to which it purportedly objected.

It is nothing less than hypocritical and politically self-serving when detractors savage the Court for activism and, at the same time, urge the appointment of judges who will import family values or any other element of a partisan agenda. Many who advocated the impeachment of Chief Justice Warren, because of the Court's development of and emphasis upon individual rights and principles of equality, seem to have been less interested in a truly restrained judiciary than in one that advanced their ideological agenda. Reference to any extraconstitutional values as a predicate for rewriting abortion law, permitting school prayer or fashioning any other constitutional law denotes subjectivism that merely has an altered focus. Urgings of restraint are especially difficult to take seriously when so obviously result-oriented.

Those who condemn activism as an encroachment upon legislative authority, to be consistent, would respect the enactments of any government which it recognizes as legitimate. It is impossible to encourage judicial disregard of apartheid laws in South Africa or objectionable laws of other recognized systems, and simultaneously rail against domestic reference to external values, without appearing to be or actually being hypocritical. Efforts to distinguish the circumstances may argue that South Africa is not governed by a system representative of most of its population, so support for judicial review which crafts principles from a moral rather than legal code and responds to pluralism is not inconsistent. Lost in that contention, however, would be the fact that until this century the majority of American citizens were not franchised, but the legitimacy of prior governmental action is not subject to dispute. The point remains that disapproval of judicial review often is tied to result rather than process, and even those who most vocally propound restraint often are closet activists.

Still, the judiciary tends to be susceptible to verbal assault whenever it asserts a principle unenumerated by the constitution and displaces legislative judgment as a consequence.[31] The judicially created right to elect an abortion is frequently adverted to as a particularly egregious instance of unprincipled activism, insofar as legislative and democratic will supposedly has been held hostage by a precept not clearly identified by the constitution itself. For many, including some who sympathize with the result, the decision epitomizes judicial activism at its worst.[32] Whether or not freedom of choice rests upon a conscientious or contrived reading of the constitution ultimately is unprovable. Incorporation of external values is an invariable dimension of constitutional law, however, and a reality that for many is difficult to reconcile with democratic expectations.

The idea that constitutional engraftments operate at parity with explicit constitutional prescriptions offends the popular image of a government of laws and evokes reminders of the dubious nature and works of natural justice. Although the most biased, prejudiced and poorly conceived judgment obviously may itself in the constitution, to hide its true nature, some theorists openly have asserted that the Court properly and overtly may reach beyond the constitution in declaring fundamental law.[33] Even pure subjectivism would not be an unadulterated evil if reference to a higher natural law might have voided the explicit protection of the slave trade originally provided by the constitution.[34]

In any event, arguments over whether the judiciary may be subjective, and if so to what extent, usually invest in the illusion that

13

a meaningful line can be drawn between what are and are not acceptable reference points. Because motive often can be disguised reasoning manipulated to achieve a predetermined result, and the judgment constitutionally wrapped, however, theories of process restraint tend to be misplaced. They disregard, moreover, the reality that open-ended terminology in an evolving society does not lend itself to criteria that can be successfully catalogued. What counts in the end, for both constitutional and democratic purposes, is whether actual results can be persuasively defended.

Judicial activism although widely condemned is not always well understood. Much criticism of activism fails to acknowledge certain exercises which are an unavoidable and indispensable feature of a constitutional society. The process of expounding and applying law by its very nature is activist. Disagreement with the results of that practice often is the real basis for objecting to a court's exercise of power. Allegations of judicial usurpation of legislative authority tend to be most impassioned when a court strikes down law supported by majoritarian sentiment or concerning a controversial subject. Decisions ordering desegregation, permitting abortions and forbidding school prayer all have elicited criticism that the Court has snubbed democratic principles and prompted initiatives to curb its authority.[35]

It is an insufficient objection, however, to protest that the judiciary is legislating. Courts make law even when they merely uphold a challenged action. Deference to legislative judgment affirms and validates whatever policy or scheme may be at issue and defines any affected rights accordingly. Whether finding an act or practice consistent with or contrary to a fundamental principle, an addition or subtraction is made to or from the body of constitutional law. In originally sustaining rather than repudiating the established custom of slavery, for instance, the Court still created a new albeit short-lived constitutional principle that blacks were not citizens and possessed no rights.[36] More pertinent in assessing judicial review, therefore, are the purpose, nature and effect of the exercise.

Legislators and judges alike are sworn to uphold the constitution.[37] Within the terms of that obligation, legislators have

14

considerable latitude to act subjectively. Thus, a legislator may vote to enact a law as a consequence of statesmanlike consideration or because he or she:

> thought the bill would provide jobs for his district, or may have wanted to make amends with a faction of his party he had alienated on another vote, or he may have been a close friend of the bill's sponsor, or he may have been repaying a favor he owed the Majority Leader, or he may have hoped the Governor would appreciate his vote and make a fundraising appearance for him, or he may have been pressured to vote for a bill he disliked by a wealthy contributor or by a flood of constituent mail, or he may have been seeking favorable publicity or he may have been reluctant to hurt the feelings of a loyal staff member who worked on the bill, or he may have been settling an old score with a legislator who opposed the bill, or he may have been mad at his wife who opposed the bill, or he may have been intoxicated, and utterly unmotivated when the vote was called, or he may have accidentally voted "yes" instead of "no", or, of course, he may have had (and very likely did have) a combination of some of the above motives.[38]

Subjective motivation is better tolerated in the legislative sphere, probably because it is assumed that deviance can be remedied at the polls. Idiosyncratic preference, however, at times is confused with activism that in a principled fashion voids legislative judgment but conflicts with popular sentiment. Failure to distinguish between the advancement of ideology tied only to personal preference and the explication of a principle with unpopular ramifications is unfair both to the institution and the constitution. In reviewing law against constitutional demands and principles that are not always self-revealing, judicial inquiry sometimes endeavors to discern values deeply rooted in the citizenry's conscience. Dissatisfaction may ensue when the selection of ideals, from which enduring principles may be constructed, chooses what an enlightened and reflective rather than a short-sighted or uninformed public would subscribe to.

The separate but equal doctrine, which constitutionalized official segregation, typifies the output of a judiciary which focused upon what proved to be underdeveloped societal values. The desegregation mandate evinces judgment tied to a higher standard of expectation. The net instructional significance of those decisions is that judicial lawmaking representing an earnest effort to discern significant values, and which makes a diligent effort to convince the citizenry of the soundness of the ideals it has selected, may rescue rather than ravage constitutional government. Despite its mistakes, the judiciary more than once has saved constitutional interests from the snares of societal conventions that would subordinate persons on the basis of race or gender, suppress diversity of expression or promote other mischief to fundamental values or concerns.

The prospect of a judicial system routinely deferential to other institutions of government and bound to apply only constitutional explications or manifest implications is scarier than the chances of unprincipled activism becoming epidemic and democratic ways being compromised. Restricting the judiciary to what the constitution textually articulates or clearly intimates essentially would gut the charter's basic guarantees which, standing alone or within the four corners of the document, signify little or nothing. Majoritarian will even if formally enacted is not necessarily congruent with the values of due process, equal protection and other majestic but textually undefined guarantees of the constitution. Jurisprudence heedless of that reality too often has been responsible for constitutional affronts. The tawdry accoutrements of institutional meekness include, among other things, slavery,[39] the separate but equal doctrine,[40] involuntary sterilization schemes,[41] capitulation to McCarthyism[42] and coerced relocation of citizens regarded as a threat to national security.[43]

Judicial assertiveness, although not always beyond reproach, has been responsible for commencing movement toward an integrated society,[44] formulating concepts of expressive and religious freedom, privacy and fairness in the criminal justice system[45] and thereby checking treacheries of majoritarianism that otherwise would traumatize important values and pluralism.

Regardless of any ambiguities or uncertainties concerning the judiciary's role at the time of the constitution's drafting, its primacy in interpreting and applying the constitution is largely beyond dispute. President Nixon challenged the premise, in seeking to withhold from the judiciary evidence that eventually led to his political demise.[46] In resisting a subpoena for White House tapes containing conversations pertaining to the burglary of Democratic National Party headquarters, Nixon asserted an "absolute privilege of confidentiality for all Presidential communications."[47] Like President Jefferson who first clashed with the judiciary in *Marbury v. Madison,* he too ultimately acknowledged the Court's paramount role. Confronted with an order that Jefferson actually might have disregarded,[48] Nixon released the Watergate tapes even at the cost of his resignation from office.

Conventional wisdom often associates restraint with deference toward legislative judgment, while activism is linked to displacement of it. Judicial restraint and activism in practice, however, are not necessarily at opposite analytical poles. Devitalized or constrained readings of liberty and equal protection, as the separate but equal doctrine evinces, can be consciously steered albeit in facially restrained fashion toward a constitutional effect as profound as a more overtly activist order to bus students for desegregation purposes. Either deference or displacement can have profound political and constitutional consequences. Whether the terms of the Fourteenth Amendment are substantively suffused or defused, the purview of rights and liberties are positively defined. If the Court refused to hear a single case or deferred to and upheld every governmental act, constitutional principles would be affirmed or aligned. Even complete passiveness, therefore, can represent activism that is subjectively motivated. Since deference in an individual instance or as a general rule may reflect concern primarily with convenience of result, concepts of restraint remain vulnerable to the forces arrayed against them. Because activism manifests itself in many shapes and stripes, and concern regarding potential abuse is present for some but not others, nonspecific complaints about it confuse rather than clarify the issue. Failure to differentiate may suggest analysis that is reflexive rather than reflective, concerned with utility of outcome rather than integrity of process or simply demagogic.

Not only is it mistaken to conclude that passivity creates no law, but restraint can function as a subtle and especially pernicious form of activism. If a judge is inclined to shape the law, so it merely reflects an interposition of personal ideology, professions of restraint afford a disguise for doing so. Such a veil sheathed the Court's decisions which upheld and fortified the institution of slavery[49] and constituted prominent waystations in the nation's march toward civil war. The infamy of those decisions, which ultimately were reversed by force of arms as well as reason, owes not just to the fact but to the manner of the Court's activism.

When a slave sued for freedom on grounds he had lived with his owner for several years in a free territory, the Court in the name of restraint rendered an opinion that remains probably the worst stain on its record. Because slaves were not recognized as citizens at the time, the case of *Scott v. Sanford*[50] could have been decided on the narrow ground that the plaintiff had no right to sue in federal court. Chief Justice Taney, in announcing the Court's decision, articulated the classic sense of judicial restraint by noting that it is not "the province of the Court to decide upon the justice or injustice, the polity or impolity of these [slavery] laws."[51] Taney, however, traveled far beyond the bounds of restraint in rendering his opinion. Instead of merely denying Scott the right to sue, he asserted that no black person, whether slave or free, could be an American citizen.[52] Taney coursed even further beyond necessary decisional premises by holding that Congress was without power to prohibit slavery.[53]

Conversion of an issue concerning the rights of a slave, into a holding denying rights to an entire race, revealed a state of mind attuned primarily to the sentiments of extreme Southern rights champions. So too did the Court's negation of congressional authority since, apart from challenges to interference with slavery, the Court prior to the Civil War consistently upheld and expanded federal powers.

The Dred Scott opinion is the unmistakable product of a majority inspired by racist ideology. Even if Taney truly had adhered to principles of restraint in upholding slavery, it is doubtful that the Court would have emerged without the enormous loss of

18

confidence in and respect for it that resulted from its ruling. The default of vision, which earned the Court its depiction as "the citadel of Slaveocracy,"[54] was compounded by the dissembling claim of restraint that masked its subjectivism. The Court expounded the seemingly restrained notion that blacks could not be recognized as citizens because the constitution's framers regarded them as inferior and conferred no rights upon them.[55] Implicit in its further determination that blacks "might justly and lawfully be reduced to slavery" were the Court's own racist convictions.[56]

Purported deference to the founding fathers did not obscure the subjective curbing of congressional power. Nor is institutional reputation salvageable on grounds the Fourteenth Amendment, which conferred citizenship on blacks, had not been adopted. The decision injected significant substantive meaning into the Fifth Amendment's due process clause.[57] It essentially constructed a fundamental right of property in a slave and interposed it as a constitutional impediment against Congress.[58] The decision reflected a prioritization of competing values that elevated slaveowner interests in liberty and property and subordinated rival concerns with liberty and equality. Even if also the product of subjectivism, a contrary result would have fashioned a more respectable legacy. The immense damage to the Court's reputation and moral authority attributable to its endorsement of slavery demonstrates that it is the nature and result of activism and not merely the process itself that is significant.

The slavery decisions, not to mention other stylings of restraint disguising ideology or subjectivism, help explain why "Every justice has been accused of legislating and everyone has joined in that accusation of others."[59] Such trading of allegations misses the more relevant point that commitment to activism or restraint does not determine whether a judge has abused his or her power to identify and develop constitutional interests. Dedication to restraint may denote an inclination to narrow or delete constitutional guarantees which, in the interest of personal liberty or equality, were designed to curb governmental power. Reluctance to invoke due process or equal protection may betoken, not restraint as a matter of principle, but restraint as a handmaiden of statism. Failure to probe outside values and engraft principles upon the constitution may amount to lawmaking by default that is both activist and mischievous.

Some fundamental principles are so taken for granted that their explicit presence in the constitution probably is assumed. Freedoms to travel or associate and rights to vote and privacy exist, however, not because of express constitutional dictate but as a consequence of judicial pronouncement.[60] Being settled now in the collective value system of the nation, their disregard in the name of judicial restraint would be no less activist than their creation and considerably more disquieting.

Persistent emphasis upon judges who will apply the law as written is mystifying. Even a cursory reading of the constitution reveals that much critical text is susceptible to varying interpretation and not amenable to mechanical implementation. The open-ended terminology of such guarantees as "freedom of speech, [and] of the press," "due process" and "equal protection," among other basic principles, invariably begets diverse understandings and should obviate much debate over the imperatives of externally value-referenced activism.

Because the injection of meaning into principles that are not self-defining is unavoidable, if the constitution is to have any meaning, theories propounding restraint at best represent a path toward devitalization and at worst a formula of political convenience. The pertinent reality, generally bypassed by calculated political rhetoric, is that external values are indispensable reference points for actuating text that neither expresses nor implies its purport. Judicial review may reflect a sincere effort to animate the constitution with values perceived as basic or a self-interested attempt to advance ideology with a ritual nod to constitutional text or notion. Because subjective intent is known for certain only to the decisionmaker, integrity of process and result in either instance may be unprovable.

Good faith in reading the constitution and determining what values should be infused into resultant constitutional law, and accountability in expounding upon, justifying, modifying and even retracting any constitutional engraftment, are more pertinent toward achieving satisfactory results than any specific formula susceptible to encapsulation. The question of whether extra-constitutional reference points are appropriate for charting constitutional principle has evoked considerable debate,[61] but it is exaggerated insofar as any decision reflects degrees of subjectivism dictated by personal orientation, experience and bias. It is doubtful that any constitutional statement is unaccompanied by reference to at least some constitutional passage. The ultimate test of any judicial pronouncement, given the difficulties of discerning actual formative influences, must be how well it persuades society of its imperatives.

The right to privacy may be viewed, for instance, as having no evident constitutional premises except those manufactured by judicial creativity. Because support for its existence and operation is consensual or close to it, its status as a right of constitutional stature is secure. A failure to be equally convincing in promulgating liberty of contract earlier this century led to its eventual devolution as a constitutional principle. The divergent results help demonstrate that actual origin of principle may be less significant than the effectiveness of its expression or societal disposition toward it. Instead of fashioning analytical guides that attempt vainly to facilitate principled results, but which have little utility beyond partisan exploitation or academic gymnastics, it may be more useful simply to consider whether a precept is capable of commanding long-term respect. Such a focus may diminish theories which excite some legalistic minds but in practice may be circumvented, subverted or manipulated. Meaningful appraisal instead would look candidly to quality and accountability of result as an important linkage to democratic consent.

The Court's identification of fundamental rights over the past few decades has been discomforting for some who regard it as a resurrection of uncontrolled and discredited concepts of natural justice.[62] Theories of natural rights are problematical, since they breed unresolvable competition between conflicting ideologies and moralities. Emphasis upon economic rights earlier this century demonstrated the hazards of translating a favored social philosophy into constitutional principle.[63] The unhappy consequences of that practice have left a strong impression upon subsequent generations of jurists who are quick to warn that the "Constitution . . . can actively intrude into . . . economic and policy matters only if [the Court] is prepared to bear enormous institutional and social costs."[64]

Contemporary formulations of constitutional principle, are accompanied by standards attempting to objectify the recognition of fundamental rights and interests. Determination of whether an interest is "implicit in the concept of ordered liberty" or central "to the traditions and conscience of our people"[65] is not without the risk of subjectivism. Standards are less instrumental in assuring principled review than, as Justice Harlan observed, respect for the teachings of history, sensitivity to the values underlying society and appreciation of the doctrines of federalism and separation of powers.[66] Such wisdom is afforded by no objective theory of review. To the contrary, professions of restraint may obscure unprincipled activism and offer as a solution what may be a problem.

The most critical determinant of sound judicial review is not adherence to a singular concept of procedural restraint or any formula that can be verbalized. The real key to a decision's quality and validity, whether it refers to or beyond the constitution, is its capacity to command societal respect. If it can, the means and sources of principle become secondary. The devolution of liberty of contract and busing to achieve equal protection testify respectively that, whether impulsive or meticulously tied to fundamental values, constitutional principles are unlikely to endure without broad and lasting assent.

Power is subject to being abused not just by the judiciary but by all institutions of government. Too often missing from assaults upon the judiciary is an appreciation of how conservative and majoritarian a force it tends to be. The reality is that no theory of review can ensure against abuse of power. A dispassionate appraisal suggests that the judiciary, despite imperfections, is subject to meaningful democratic influences and institutional checks and balances that work more effectively than is commonly recognized. From endorsement of slavery and fabrication of the separate but equal doctrine to the shaping of First Amendment doctrine that accommodated McCarthyism and curbing of busing as a desegregation remedy, the Court has evinced a sensitivity to popular inclinations and has generally exercised its power along majoritarian lines.

# References

1. *Marbury v. Madison*, 5 U.S. (1 Cranch) 137, 163 (1803).
2. *Id.*
3. *See infra* Chapter Two.
4. The Court specifically has resisted opportunities to examine and vitalize the Ninth Amendment, which reserves all rights not constitutionally enumerated to the people, and privileges and immunities clause of the Fourteenth Amendment. See *Griswold v. Connecticut*, 381 U.S. 479 (1965); (Ninth Amendment); Slaughter-House Cases, 83 U.S. (16 Wall.) 36 (1873) (Privileges and Immunities).
5. U.S. CONST., amend. XIV (1868).
6. *Buck v. Bell*, 274 U.S. 200, 208 (1927).
7. *Plessy v. Ferguson*, 163 U.S. 537 (1896).
8. *Brown v. Board of Education*, 347 U.S. 483 (1954).
9. *Regents of the University of California v. Bakke*, 438 U.S. 265 (1978).
10. *City of Richmond v. I.A. Croson Company*, 109 S Ct. 706 (1989).
11. For a representative sampling of works propounding theories of and justification for judicial restraint, *see, e.g.,* A. BICKEL, THE LEAST DANGEROUS BRANCH (1962); L. LEVY, THE BILL OF RIGHTS (1958); Bork, *Neutral Principles and Some First Amendment Problems*, 47 IND. L.J. 1 (1971); Wechsler, *Toward Neutral Principles of Constitutional Law*, 73 HARV. L. REV. 1 (1959).
12. *See infra* Chapter Five.
13. Radio Address by President Franklin D. Roosevelt, March 9, 1937, *reprinted in* G. GUNTHER, CONSTITUTIONAL LAW 129 (1985).
14. B. SCHWARTZ, SWANN'S WAY, 188–89 (1986).
15. Vice President George Bush, Second Presidential Debate, October 13, 1988.
16. Legislative efforts to prohibit court-ordered busing have yet to succeed, although the Senate in 1982 adopted such a provision and a Senate Subcommittee approved one as recently as 1984. *See* G. GUNTHER, *supra*, note 13 at 719–20. Senator Helms, responding to the failure of his proposal for curbing court jurisdiction over school prayer, commented that "[t]here is more than one way to skin a cat, and there is more than one way for Congress to provide a check on arrogant Supreme Court Justices who routinely distort the Constitution to suit their own notions of public policy." 130 CONG. REC. § 2901.

17. U.S. CONST., Art. 1, § 3.
18. *Id.*, art. 1, § 8[3].
19. *See, e.g., Hodel v. Virginia Surface Mining Association*, 452 U.S. 264 (1981) (environmental); *Perez v. United States*, 402 U.S. 146 (1971) (criminal); *Katzenbach v. McClung*, 379 U.S. 294 (1964) (civil rights).
20. Such cases arise under U.S. CONST., amend. I.
21. Such cases arise under U.S. CONST., amend. VI.
22. Such cases arise under U.S. CONST., amend. VIII.
23. Such cases arise under U.S. CONST., amend. VIII.
24. Such issues arise under U.S. CONST., amend. I.
25. Such issues arise under U.S. CONST., amend. I.
26. U.S. CONST., amend. XIV.
27. Hutcheson, Jr., *The Judgment Intuitive: The Function of the 'Hunch' in Judicial Decision*, 14 CORNELL L.Q. 274 (1929).
28. *See* A.T. MASON, THE SUPREME COURT FROM TAFT TO WARREN 37–38 (1968).
29. *See infra* Chapter Five.
30. *See* Goldman, *Reorganizing the Judiciary: The First Term Appointments*, 68 JUDICATURE 313, 316 (1985), Brownstein, *With or Without Supreme Court Changes, Reagan Will Reshape the Federal Bench*, 49 NAT'L. J. 2338, 2340 (1984).
31. *See supra* note 11.
32. *See infra* Chapter Six.
33. *See, e.g.,* Grey, Do We Have an Unwritten Constitution? 27 STAN. L.REV. 703, 706 (1975).
34. *See* U.S. CONST., art. I, § 9.
35. *See supra* note 16.
36. *See Scott v. Sanford*, 60 U.S. (19 How.) 393 (1857).
37. *See Marbury v. Madison*, 5 U.S. (Cranch) at 180.
38. *Edwards v. Aguillard*, 107 S.Ct. 2573, 2605 (1987) (Scalia, J., dissenting).
39. *See Scott v. Sanford*, 60 U.S. (19 How.) 393.
40. *See Plessy v. Ferguson*, 163 U.S. 537.
41. *See Buck v. Bell*, 274 U.S. 200 (1927).
42. *See* J. NOWAK, R. ROTUNDA, J. YOUNG, CONSTITUTIONAL LAW, §1614, at 859–62 (1986).
43. *See Korematsu v. United States*, 323 U.S. 214 (1944).
44. *See Brown v. Board of Education*, 347 U.S. 483.
45. *See, e.g., Miranda v. Arizona*, 384 U.S. 436 (1966) (rights of the accused); *Griswold v. Connecticut*, 381 U.S 479 (right of privacy); *Brown v. Board of Education*, 347 U.S. 483 (desegregation); *Everson v. Board of Education*, 330 U.S. 1 (1947) (wall between church and state); *Near v. Minnesota*, 283 U.S. 697 (1931) (liberty of press means immunity from prior restraint).
46. *See United States v. Nixon*, 418 U.S. 683 (1974).
47. *Id.* at 703.
48. *See infra* Chapter Two.
49. *See, e.g., Scott v. Sanford*, 60 U.S. (19 How.) 393; *Moore v. Illinois*, 55 U.S. (How.) 13 (1853); *Jones v. Van Zandt*, 46 U.S. (5 How.) 215 (1847); *Prigg v. Pennsylvania*, 41 U.S. (16 Pet.) 539 (1842); *Queen v. Hepburn*, 11 U.S. (7 Cranch) 290 (1813).

50. 60 U.S. (19 How.) 393.

51. *Scott v. Sanford*, 60 U.S. (19 How.) at 405, 426.

52. *Id.* at 421.

53. *Id.* at 452.

54. A.T. MASON, *supra* note 28, at 16.

55. *Scott v. Sanford*, 46 U.S. (19 How.) at 404–12.

56. *Id.* at 407.

57. *Id.* at 450–52.

58. *Id.* at 451.

59. R. JACKSON, THE SUPREME COURT IN THE AMERICAN SYSTEM OF GOVERNMENT 80 (1955).

60. *Zobel v. Williams*, 457 U.S. 55 (1982) (right to travel); *Griswold v. Connecticut*, 381 U.S. 479 (1965) (right of privacy); *Baker v. Carr*, 369 U.S. 186 (1962); *NAACP v. Alabama*, 357 U.S. 449 (1958) (freedom of association).

61. *See supra* note 33.

62. *See, e.g., Griswold v. Connecticut*, 381 U.S. at 507 (Black, J. dissenting).

63. *United States Trust Company v. New Jersey*, 431 U.S. 1, 62 (1978) (Brennan, J., dissenting).

64. *Id.*

65. Such focal points originally were employed in determining whether a guarantee expressed in the Bill of Rights, and thus protected against federal incursion, is incorporated through the Fourteenth Amendment and thereby also made applicable against the states. *See Duncan v. Louisiana*, 391 U.S. 145, 149 n.14 (1968); *Palko v. Connecticut*, 302 U.S. 319, 324–25 (1937). They have evolved largely in response to an identified need to avoid subjectivism in both appearance and reality.

66. *See Griswold v. Connecticut*, 381 U.S. at 501 (Harlan, J., concurring).

# Two

# John Marshall, the Original Activist

For true advocates of judicial dormancy, history provides a dismaying record. Despite the rhetoric of critics and even its own opinions, the Supreme Court consistently has worked to identify objectives and values which although not explicated or implicated by constitutional text have become the predicate for fundamental law. The political and legal culture from which the nation and constitution emerged was hospitable toward and even facilitative of such activism, as the framers knowingly deferred judgment on certain issues in the interest of forming a union. Resolution of slavery in unqualified terms prohibiting or permitting it, for instance, would have split the Constitutional Convention and doomed ratification. A final decision upon constitutionality thus was expressly reserved for subsequent generations which, after 1808, could consider banning the import of slaves.[1]

Likewise deferred by conscious design if not explicit terms was the ultimate meaning of basic guarantees recited by the Bill of Rights. An enumeration of safeguards that would secure individual liberties against government encroachment also was a concession to the imperatives of ratification. The consequent itemization of rights and liberties, including a provision that those not enumerated were reserved to the people, created only a textual starting point from which substantive meaning would have to evolve. Vitalization of any of those guarantees required the importation of values from

27

which meaningful principles could be constructed. It is misleading, therefore, when self-proclaimed exponents of restraint advocate interpretation of the constitution as written or insist upon what its creators clearly intended. Discernment of what the framers thought, said and did is a largely vain assignment if conceived as a primary means for constitutional animation. Given the confidentiality of convention proceedings, variances of original opinion and purpose and problems and issues never even contemplated at the time of drafting, a guiding purpose tends to be indeterminable or nonexistent. What is evident from the composition process and consequent terms of the constitution itself is that the framers inscribed an invitation for activist vitalization.

The unfinished nature of the constitution's terms and provisions owed not just to practical considerations but philosophical influences. Central to the conception and chartering of the American Republic was the prominent Eighteenth Century notion that people had natural rights derived from God. The American Revolution represented the crest of a political philosophy that considered citizens to be "free people, claiming their rights as derived from the laws of nature, and not as the gift of the" state.[2]

Creation of a new nation institutionalized John Locke's philosophy of natural law. Locke maintained that persons entering into a social compact for self-governance did not divest themselves of the fundamental rights and liberties they enjoyed in a previously ungoverned or natural condition.[3] The nation's founding and formative documents are suffused with references to natural law reflecting the philosophical impulses of the time. The Continental Congress of 1774 declared that basic rights, including life, liberty and property, flowed from "the immutable laws of nature."[4]

Both the Virginia Declaration of Rights of 1776[5] and Massachusetts Constitution of 1780[6] identified freedom and equality as "natural," "inalienable" and "inherent." The Declaration of Independence consolidated those precepts by proclaiming the "self-evident truths (of) equality" and "unalienable Rights ... [of] Life, Liberty and the Pursuit of Happiness."[7] It further embellished them with references to the creation of legitimate government "from the consent of the governed" and its existence "to secure those rights."[8] The constitution, as a means of facilitating "a more perfect Union" and "the Blessings of Liberty,"[9] represents the documentary end point of a heritage not merely comfortable with but assuming the existence of basic rights beyond those prescribed by official charter.

Especially given the secrecy of the drafting proceedings, a case for judicial activism cannot be conclusively grounded in the debates accompanying the constitution's framing and ratification. It is equally true, however, that the record is bereft of clear-cut support for competing arguments. The absence of specific original intents, however, does not preclude claims of their existence. More often than not, such assertions have little validity.

Diggings into past purpose frequently unearth conflicting aims which result in selection of a design most serviceable for a particular agenda. A focus upon intent at a formative and largely experimental stage, moreover, may result in poor guidance if it discounts or disregards how subsequent experience may alter original expectations or contemplations. Determining any precise sense of judicial review generally subscribed to by the framers is complicated by the absence of a clear record before, during or after the convention. In the words of one observer, "The people who say the framers intended [judicial review] are talking nonsense, and the people who say they did not intend it are talking nonsense."[10] Still, it may be possible to draw from original actions if not words some generalizations regarding the anticipated nature of the judiciary. Even if impossible to prove that the judiciary's eventual functions were precisely contemplated, the founders created the framework from which its role could evolve.

Arguments that an activist judiciary was not in the original cards dealt by the framers sometimes advert to their rejection of a proposal that would have enabled the Supreme Court, like the president, to exercise a veto.[11] It is mistaken, however, to infer from that decision any animosity toward judicial review as it has developed. Although the proposal was rebuffed in part because the judiciary's consequent authority would have intimated a wisdom superior to any other branch of government,[12] objections were not necessarily hostile toward an institution that would construct principles against which official action would be measured. To the contrary, concern was expressed that the "Supreme Judiciary [required] the confidence of the people" and would be jeopardized if the Court routinely was pitted against the popularly elected legislature.[13]

The worries that led toward a less confrontational function, and a role more insulated from raw politics, are irrelevant in assessing the propriety of review that measures legislation against constitutional standards. Given a recognition that the constitutionality of laws would "come before the Judge in their proper official character,"[14] and sensitivity to the identified need for popular confidence in the judiciary, eventual exercise of judicial power to review federal and state law does not lack a creditable connection. Whether specific intent for such a function is provable or not now is largely immaterial. It is a power established nearly two centuries ago, when incidentally most of the constitution's architects were still alive, by the Court itself. Thanks to Chief Justice Marshall, as discussed below, the practice is as entrenched now as any principle etched in the constitution itself.

Even if it could be established that the framers contemplated a judiciary authorized to hold all government accountable not only to constitutional text but its own constitutional engraftments, debate still might persist over permissible reference points for creating fundamental law. Contemporary scholarship has focused considerable attention upon whether principles must be fashioned from concepts clearly developed from within the four corners of the document or may be imported from external value systems.

One of the ironies of originalism is that those who favor reading the words and minds of the framers as a narrow interpretive device must account for the fact that many of the constitution's architects subscribed to theories of natural justice. It is not unreasonable to infer that many of those who endorsed the Declaration of Independence as a manifestly natural law document, and contributed later to the constitution's creation, regarded the nation's charter document as paramount human law but still subordinate to natural law. If so, they would not have even blushed at the notion of pronouncing as fundamental a principle that was neither explicated nor obviously implicated by constitutional text. Given a dominant philosophy of the time, which regarded personal rights as pre-existent and paramount to organized government and its dictates, conditions probably were more friendly toward value importation then than now.

Shortly after the constitution's ratification, the Court began debate over the nature and scope of fundamental rights and the judiciary's role in discerning and effectuating freedoms and liberties not textually identified. It is a dispute that is rekindled every time the Court delineates a right not explicitly enumerated by the constitution itself and interposes it to negate government action.

In *Calder v. Bull*,[15] Justice Iredell sounded a theory of judicial restraint that has been repeated many times since. Iredell asserted that reliance on natural law to invalidate the acts of other governmental branches was extraconstitutional and undermined the democratic process.[16] Although acknowledging the Court's power to invalidate federal or state action conflicting with textually palpable constitutional restrictions, Iredell asserted that enforcement of natural law would hold democratic principles hostage to the personal ideology of individual justices.[17]

Iredell's position would be reconstituted, a century and a half later, when Justice Black objected to recognition of a right of privacy. Black considered the Court's privacy pronouncement as a product of natural justice. Traveling the same path forged by Iredell, he concluded government could invade a person's privacy "unless prohibited by some specific constitutional" provision.[18] Like much modern criticism of activism, Iredell's position seems to reflect mistrust of the judiciary and concern that it will use its power subjectively and to the detriment of democratic ways. Black reiterated the concern in observing that natural justice "require[s] judges to determine what is or is not unconstitutional on the basis of their own appraisal of what laws are unwise or unnecessary."[19]

Justice Chase, in contrast, asserted that the citizenry vested government with power limited by both constitutional and natural law.[20] From Chase's point of view, the judiciary's protection of natural or unenumerated rights from governmental interference vindicated rather than retarded the citizenry's will.[21] Chase's sentiment is seldom openly embraced or echoed. In identifying fundamental rights not specifically enumerated by the constitution, the Court works toward advancing an image that it does "not sit as a super-legislature to determine the wisdom, need, and propriety of laws."[22] Not infrequently, it takes considerable pains to create an appearance that the constitution is speaking for itself, by means of penumbras, emanations or other internal design, rather than candidly acknowledging that the Court determines the document's message pursuant to the values imported and consequent grafting of principles.

The debate commenced by Iredell and Chase has persisted over the years, with the Court generally professing adherence to the Iredell position but often acting in a fashion reflecting the influence and vitality of Chase's views. Even in one of the most criticized episodes of constructing principle from external values, when it advanced economic rights during the first part of this century pursuant to concepts of marketplace freedom, the Court prefaced decisions with the observation that it should not second-guess legislative wisdom.[23] Such conflict between word and deed suggests an institutional sensitivity to its function in a democratic society, but also reveals a hypocrisy and deception that merits reproach.

Philosophical debate notwithstanding, the vitality of natural justice was evident in the early deeds and assumptions of some courts. Instances abound in which the judiciary, consistent with natural law premises, presumed the existence of unwritten guarantees precluding certain forms of government action. A New York court in 1822, for instance, heard arguments that the state had effected a taking of private property even though the Fifth Amendment[24] pertained only to the federal government and the state constitution had no comparable due process provision. Pursuant to what it described simply as "a great and fundamental [albeit unspecified] principle of government,"[25] the Court ordered the state to pay just compensation for any private land taken for public use.[26] It thus evinced a readiness to find "any law violating the [unenumerated] principle . . . a nullity, as it [would be] against natural rights and justice."[27]

Other courts also found natural law to be a convenient source of principle no less available than or effective as enumerated rights in blunting state action. A South Carolina court found a statute to be "against common right and reason, as well as against *magna charta* and thus *ipso facto*, void."[28] Even the Supreme Court flirted with natural justice, as Chief Justice Marshall found a state's revocation of a land grant invalid "either by general principles which are common to our free institutions, or by the particular provisions of the constitution."[29]

The conspicuous weakness of any natural law theory is that its validity rests upon subjective belief or assumption rather than objective standard. More akin to morality than positive law, it is susceptible to discrete or varying rather than uniform subscription. Natural justice in contemporary times may emphasize equality, but at an earlier point in time would have regarded inequality as a natural condition. Thus, the Court could uphold slavery on the basis that blacks were "so far inferior" to whites "that they had no rights which the white man was bound to respect."[30] The divergent and evolutionary nature of values explains not only why racial inferiority was once assumed but why slavery was a natural condition in the mind of Aristotle[31] and apartheid is the official order in South Africa.

The operation of natural law manifestly contemplates the exercise of subjectivism for better and for worse. The premise that democracy is superior to any other political system, and consequent standards against which judicial review is measured, are themselves an extension of nonuniversal values reflecting moral judgment and expounding what is perceived as rather than demonstrably natural. Reference to extraconstitutional values does not necessarily translate into uncontrolled subjectivism. At minimum, the judiciary's introduction of an externally referenced value requires a compelling reason that ultimately must prove satisfactory to the citizenry. Such accountability is crucial, as a history including pronouncements on slavery and economic freedom has demonstrated, if its pronouncements and function are to be taken seriously.

In any event, concepts of natural law were significantly invested in during the nation's early years. It is those who begrudge the judiciary's capacity to enrich the constitution's fabric with externally referenced principles, whose sentiments seem to have coursed most radically.

If not conclusively set by any actual dialogue among the framers, the capacity of the judiciary to spin law from values at least was facilitated by the tone of debate over the Bill of Rights. Adoption of the first ten amendments to the constitution reflected a Federalist concession to the argument that explicit safeguards for individual rights and liberties were necessary. A reservation of "powers not delegated to the United States by the constitution . . . to the people"[32] thus proved critical in effectuating a compromise between rival political philosophies and securing ratification of the constitution. Inclusion of the Ninth Amendment as a repository for unenumerated rights assuaged concerns that itemization would invite later interpretations of an exclusive recital.

Modern discomfort with or resistance to constitutional grafting[33] demonstrates the foresight of the framers' apprehensions. The Court's refusal to explore the Ninth Amendment in any meaningful fashion also suggests that contemporary jurisprudence is considerably less activist than what the founding fathers in crafting the provision possibly contemplated. It is at least peculiar that one of the guarantees, upon which the constitution's fate most hinged, has been studiously ignored since. Even if the Ninth Amendment has not proved in practice to be the storehouse of rights and freedoms that it was in theory, an institution nonetheless evolved with the responsibility for identifying and asserting enumerated and unenumerated rights.

The power of judicial review emerged from the postratification interaction of individuals who had participated actively in or observed closely the emergence of the constitution. Contours of the nation's government thus continued to be shaped by the political disputes that persisted long after the framers left Philadelphia. Chief Justice Marshall had the good fortune to lead the Court at a time when he could write on a virtually clean slate and mostly establish rather than be bound by precedent.

Marshall, an ardent Federalist and disciple and biographer of George Washington, was a fierce advocate of nationalist policies. His sense that the nation's future viability rested upon effective capital formation and economic growth accounted for a judicial philosophy that favored economic rights and was hostile to state interference with private productive activity. Under less ideologically focused direction, the Court may have been more inclined to drift than steer. During the decade before his arrival, the Court had functioned in considerable disarray and with a sense of impotency. Difficult working conditions, that included travel over poor roads to preside over distant circuit court proceedings, complicated the assemblage of strong legal talent and impaired effective institutional organization. The first chief justice, John Jay, refused reappointment to the Court on grounds the institution had no real authority or stature.[34]

Upon assuming control, Marshall discouraged dissent so the Court would speak in a single and more resonant voice and staked what has proved to be its lasting claim to power. During his tenure as Chief Justice, the Court's opinions largely reflected his Federalist values and desire for a powerful central government capable of promoting a vibrant national economy.

The Marshall Court over more than three decades invalidated only one federal law.[35] Its record, however, testifies less to restraint than to the nature of Marshall's agenda. Deferential readings of congressional power to regulate commerce and enact legislation that was "necessary and proper" expanded the national government's authority and thereby advanced his Federalist vision of strong and viable central rule. Marshall's review of federal powers in such a generous fashion demonstrates how deference or passivity toward other branches of government can be as much a facilitator of ideology or values as the more noticeable variant of activism which collides with official judgment. Even the one instance when Marshall invalidated a federal statute, in *Marbury v. Madison*,[36] remained consistent with his Federalist visions.

The overtly activist nature of the *Marbury* decision was rooted in the political conflict between Federalists and Republicans. When John Adams and Thomas Jefferson were elected president and vice president respectively in 1796, both may have hoped for the cooperative working relationship they enjoyed while drafting the Declaration of Independence. During the last few years of the Eighteenth Century, however, partisanship rose to feverish levels and the political climate became dominated by acrimony. Adams' Federalist Party portrayed Jefferson's Republican Party as the American equivalent of the radical French, while Republicans depicted the Federalists as descendants of the British elite. Following enactment of the Alien and Sedition Acts, which essentially were Federalist initiatives to curb political dissent by criminalizing it,[37] an especially bitter election campaign eventuated in 1800. From that sour atmosphere, the case of *Marbury v. Madison* emerged.

The controversy represented the final major collision between Federalist ideology and the rising tide of Jeffersonianism. Having lost the presidential election of 1800, the Federalists in their final days of control over the executive and legislative branches contrived to maintain a grip upon power.[38] Foremost in their strategy was permeating the judiciary with Federalist sympathizers. Marshall's appointment as Chief Justice, after Jefferson's election but before his inauguration, was part of that plan. The Federalist effort to pack the Court, and extend ideological influence beyond the actual term of the Adams administration, constituted a practice that has been commonly resorted to since.[39]

As noted in the previous chapter, judicial appointments calculated to advance a particular agenda are a norm in American politics. To the extent court-packing represents an effort to negate the influence of a future or incoming administration representing a popular will, it helps demonstrate that antidemocratic potential is not exclusive to the judiciary. The outgoing Federalist Congress also reduced the size of the Court, thereby intending to impede the new administration's ability to make its own assignments. Simultaneously, Congress expanded the federal circuit and appellate courts, created new justice of the peace slots in Washington, D.C., and confirmed the appointment of Federalists in those positions.[40]

Given Jefferson's understandable hostility toward the scheme, it was imperative for the Federalists to commission the judges before his inauguration. The rush to confirm the so-called "midnight judges" was overseen by Marshall who, despite having commenced service as Chief Justice, continued as Secretary of State and retained responsibility for executing and delivering the judicial commissions. Despite Federalist efforts, a few appointees did not receive their commissions before Jefferson took office. When the new president refused to forward the remaining certifications, one of the uncommissioned appointees, William Marbury, filed an original action with the Supreme Court asking it to order delivery of his commission. Marshall thus had the opportunity to resolve to his liking the controversy he had helped create.

The manifest conflict of interest presented by Marshall's simultaneous executive and judicial actions did not deter him from participating in the decision, actually authoring the opinion and thereby capitalizing upon the chance to define the judiciary's power. The chief justice could not have been insensitive to questions of impropriety, as evidenced by his recusal some years later from a case in which he had an economic interest.[41]

Ideological activism and any ethical impropriety aside, *Marbury v. Madison* emerged and endures as what "has been deemed by great English speaking Courts an indispensable, implied characteristic of a written Constitution."[42] Its overt political ambitiousness notwithstanding, the decision usually is referred to in tones of reverence rather than as an object of disrepute. The Court declared for itself the power to measure executive and legislative action against the constitution and invalidate policies adjudged in conflict with the fundamental law of the land.[43] It is that substantive consequence, rather than dubious influences upon its judgment, which constitutes *Marbury v. Madison's* chief remembrance and vitality.

The Court's arrogation of power was unashamedly activist but at the same time sensitively couched to preempt a Jeffersonian backlash. Establishing the judiciary's authority, when it was evident that the president would have ignored any order to deliver the commission, was a delicate exercise. Marshall found that Marbury had a vested right to the commission and that the executive was subject to constitutional limits identified by the Court. Knowing that Jefferson rejected such an expansive notion of review, however, the Chief Justice established the judiciary's authority without igniting an interbranch confrontation that would eviscerate it. By finding the Judiciary Act of 1789 unconstitutional, insofar as it vested the Court with original jurisdiction, he foreclosed a remedy for Marbury and thereby avoided direct conflict with the executive.[44]

Because the immediate interests of Jefferson and his allies were unaffected, Marshall effectively defused serious political opposition to the judiciary's self-announced power. Republican satisfaction with the practical resolution of the appointment controversy may not have fully appreciated the more profound contribution Marshall had made to the Federalist cause. Although Marbury's interests may have been sacrificed, the long-term political gain exceeded the proximate cost. The loss of a few Federalist judges and their potential influence paled in significance to enshrinement of the constitution as paramount law and establishment of judicial supremacy in reviewing it.

Neither the constitution's preeminent status nor the judiciary's role as its ultimate enforcer was ordained by charter or precedent. It also is unclear, as noted previously, that judicial review of executive or legislative action was anticipated by the founders. Marshall, however, did not try to prove his conclusions by references to constitutional specifics or original intent. The judicial power, as he delineated it, constituted not merely a definition but veritable seizure of authority.

As a model for future exercises of judicial power, Marshall's opinion demonstrated how the importation of external values is essential to the constitution's vitality and why diverse interpretations and subjective maneuverings are inevitable. The Judiciary Act of 1789 was subject to a principled reading, for instance, that would have begotten a different result than Marshall's. Rather than deferring to the legislative judgment responsible for its passage, Marshall construed Article III of the constitution as conclusively fixing the limits of the Court's original jurisdiction.[45] Article III vested the Court with original jurisdiction "In all Cases affecting Ambassadors, other public Ministers and Consuls, and those in which a State shall be a Party, . . . [but] in all the other cases mentioned, [gave it] appellate jurisdiction."[46] Marshall determined that the legislature could not augment the Court's power to entertain original actions.[47] Marbury's request for relief, pursuant to the Judiciary Act's provision for a writ of mandamus to federal officers, thus was denied for lack of jurisdiction.

Because the constitution's conferral of jurisdiction contained no negative or restrictive terms, it reasonably could have been concluded that Congress could augment Article III powers. If regarded as a supplement to Article III's delineation of judicial power, the enactment thus might have been adjudged consonant with rather than contrary to the constitution. In declaring an inconsistency when one did not have to be found, Marshall effectuated the first judicial preemption of congressional action.

Apart from recusal because of a conflict of interest and a legitimate alternative statutory construction, other invitations existed to travel a different or less adventurous analytical route. Logic would have supported a conclusion that Marbury's right to a commission did not vest until delivered. So too would the principle of avoiding constitutional questions whenever possible. Although a policy of "strict necessity in disposing of constitutional issues" traces back almost to the Court's first term,[48] it would be unreasonable to expect the founders and their contemporaries, many of whom lived well into the Nineteenth Century, not to explicate and gloss the law that they had crafted. Several of the framers, for instance, wrote or spoke forcefully on slavery and church and state concerns in an effort to influence the direction of constitutional principle.

Political thought at times took some unusual partisan twists. The idea of a national bank was a decidedly Federalist notion which, when first proposed in 1791 by Hamilton, caused Madison and others in Congress to object on grounds the constitution did not specifically provide for it. A couple of decades later, it was Madison and a Republican Congress that created a national bank as a means of providing centralized economic development and stability. Republican enactment of an essentially Federalist concept, without reservations about its constitutional propriety, demonstrates how principles even if tagged as basic still could be fluid. Marshall, like other figures whose influence in shaping the nation's destiny was magnified by the absence of constitutional precedent, seems to have functioned in an atmosphere that was hospitable toward doctrinal experimentation, creativity and flexibility.

A more cautious approach to the Marbury dispute also might have regarded it not as a separation of powers question but a political issue resolvable only by the executive branch. Marshall rejected that principle of nonjusticiability, sometimes used to avoid questions of power concerning another branch of government,[49] in favor of seizing a more politically enticing opportunity. Although recognizing that executive action pursuant to specifically assigned powers may be beyond judicial purview, Marshall emphasized that other presidential deeds were not beyond the ken of the Court.[50] The principle consistently has been respected even by those who subsequently have disputed it. When the Court unanimously ruled that executive privilege did not immunize President Nixon's Watergate tapes from compulsory process, it reaffirmed the precept that Marshall was not bound by any set principle to fashion.[51] Nixon's compliance accordingly reaffirmed the judiciary's primacy in discerning and declaring constitutional meaning.

Given the circumstances from which *Marbury v. Madison* emerged and the influences that shaped its outcome, it is not unfair to regard the opinion as the denouement of a cunning Federalist scheme to neutralize the impact of ideological rivals. The case presented an attractive if not ideal opportunity to advance a particular vision of judicial power and general governance. In effectuating that agenda, Marshall creatively surmounted if not cavalierly disregarded the diverse impediments to resolving the case in a fashion which advanced Federalist thinking.

Marshall's concept of judicial review was not preordained by the constitution, which confers no explicit or indisputable power upon the judiciary to void legislative or executive action. Notwithstanding competing notions of judicial power which may have existed before or in opposition to Marshall's pronouncement, however, it is his vision that was indelibly etched and passed forward.

Even if the legacy is of calculating and desperate politicians, working to perpetuate a power base that might negate or dilute emerging popular sentiment, the decision is now revered as a towering landmark and entrenched as a virtually unassailable principle of constitutional governance. Recognition of the constitution as the supreme law, coupled with the judiciary's authority to define conclusively "what the law is,"[52] established a functional responsibility that if anything has been expanded since. When the order to desegregate public schools prompted resistance in the South during the 1950s, including state efforts to nullify the decision, the Court declared its constitutional pronouncements to be "the supreme law of the land."[53] The executive's dispatch of federal troops to enforce the desegregation order demonstrated that it is not only the constitution but the Court's rendition of constitutional law that has become regarded as paramount.

Although probably Marshall's best known decision, *Marbury v. Madison* was not the only occasion upon which he used the judicial power to forward his Federalist vision. Several critical opportunities arose during his long service as Chief Justice to advance the nationalist values which he subscribed to and expounded. It was Marshall's abiding sense that the union's enduring vitality was contingent upon efficient capital formation, economic growth and cooperation among the states and respect for property rights. Three major cases illustrate his forceful ways in responding to state action that he perceived as an encumbrance upon private enterprise or impediment to a strong national identity in both political and economic terms.

Marshall's valuation of property rights was evident in *Dartmouth College v. Woodward*,[54] when the Court was called upon to determine whether a state could transform a private college into a public one by legislative decree. Although conceding that the constitution's protection against any "Law impairing the obligation of Contracts"[55] probably was directed toward private agreements, Marshall nonetheless expanded its ambit to include a state charter.[56] Acknowledgment that the constitution in precise terms did not secure a corporate charter awarded by the state from subsequent legislative interference did not distract him from his broader Federalist vision.

The practical effect of Marshall's decision was that emerging corporations, then establishing the foundation of an industrial base and national distribution system, could rely indefinitely upon the privileges conferred upon them by their charters. The ruling enhanced the power and independence of private enterprise and helped the modern corporation evolve into a pervasive economic force. It also established further precedent for weaving constitutional law from threads not explicated or inarguably implicated by the document itself.

Equally pertinent to Marshall's nationalist priorities was the effective operation of a national bank, which became jeopardized by state attempts to tax and regulate it. A national bank, which provided credit, a common currency and centralized economic direction, was controversial in both its initial and subsequent incarnations. The First and Second National Banks both evoked objections on grounds that the constitution did not specifically provide for their creation. When Maryland imposed a tax on a branch of the bank in Baltimore, the Court was confronted with questions of whether Congress had power to create the bank and whether the states could regulate a federal agency.

The issues raised in *McCulloch v. Maryland*[57] implicated both the federal government's power to create and foster national policy and the states' capacity to debilitate its coherent formulation and application. Although conceding the lack of any specific constitutional provision for a national bank, Marshall again was not deterred by the terminological void. Rather, he inferred the necessary authority from Congress' general powers and the "great objects" for which the constitution and resulting federal government was created.[58] The challenge to the bank was based in part upon a narrow reading of the "necessary and proper" clause[59] which, if so interpreted, would have allowed Congress to enact only those laws indispensable to the exercise of its enumerated powers and cramped severely its latitude in selecting regulatory means best suited for effectuating regulatory objectives.

Allowing Congress to use any means not specifically prohibited by or inconsistent with the constitution's spirit or letter represented a definition of authority that was as generous toward the federal government as it was niggardly toward the states. Such a delineation was essential if, consistent with Federalist visions, national government was to rule effectively and comprehensively. The power "to establish post offices" if interpreted in a sparing fashion, as Marshall noted, would have supported only "the single act of making the establishment."[60] Powers inferred from that enumerated authority, however, allowed carriage of the mail and sanctions against those who interfered with or misused it.[61] Marshall's determination, that Congress' authority to charter a national bank could be inferred as a necessary and proper means for effectuating its general powers,[62] represented a further infusion into the constitution of values borrowed from Federalist ideology.

Recognizing that a state's power to tax the national government represented the power to destroy it, Marshall tied federal authority to the consent of the people rather than the states.[63] Although not a consensually subscribed to notion at the time, and not conclusively decided until the end of the Civil War, his depiction of the federal government's authority forwarded the inexorable advance of nationalist philosophy. By refusing to hold national powers hostage to the competing agenda of state's rightists, and concluding that federal powers derived from the people rather than the states,[64] Marshall placed the federal government on a footing that ultimately enabled it to survive parochial sniping and factionalism and extend its political and social policies as a matter of prerogative rather than consent.

The Federalist objective of a strong and viable national economy probably was advanced most eminently by Marshall's broad delineation of Congress' power to regulate commerce. Prior to *Gibbons v. Ogden*,[65] it was unclear whether navigation was included within the definition of commerce. When a steamboat company challenged New York's award of a monopoly to a competing firm, however, the Court had an opportunity to establish the meaning of commerce in expansive terms. Marshall declared the commerce power to be plenary and subject to no limitations other than those prescribed by the constitution itself.[66]

The interpretation translated into virtually complete deference to federal regulation of commerce among and within states. Notions of purely intrastate commerce were narrowed to the point of nonexistence by the determination that such activity could not even remotely affect other states.[67] The broad denomination of commerce was retreated from a century later when the Court worked to secure private enterprise against popularly inspired reforms.[68]

History suggests, as discussed in Chapter Five, that the Court would have served itself and the nation better by adhering to Marshall's formulations. Much of Marshall's original premise, and the substance of his concern with preventing state and regional factionalism and protectionism, resurfaced eventually as a predicate for modern interpretation of federal power to regulate commerce.[69] Contemporary federal civil rights legislation, criminal law and environmental regulation owe much of their existence to Congress' power to regulate interstate commerce and their survival to the Court's reiteration of the federal government's extensive reach.[70]

Although sometimes structured in terms of effectuating the constitution's "great objects" or following its implications, Marshall's decisions in reality are the product of values drawn not from the document but gleaned from Federalist ideology and appended to it. Political doctrine transformed into constitutional law, by a process of engraftment upon the charter rather than explication or invariable implication by the document itself, thus helped facilitate the emergence of a national economy and a powerful central government.

Even if begotten by partisanship and personal vision, Marshall's aggressive exercises of power established the Court as a permanently activist political force. It is difficult to envision an institution of governance, with ultimate power to interpret and declare the law, being anything less. The acceptability of Marshall's decisions, like later rulings, however, is tied less to concepts of activism and restraint than to public perceptions of acceptability and desirability. The force of Marshall's articulation of judicial authority has been enhanced rather than eroded by the passage of time. As noted, the Court more than a century later adverted to *Marbury v. Madison* as authority for the claim that its constitutional enunciations were "the supreme law of the land."[71]

This proposition was challenged by the Reagan Administration, which suggested distinguishing "the constitution which is the law, ... [from] the decisions of the Court."[72] Such a distinction would allow the Supreme Court to bind the parties in a case and the executive branch for enforcement purposes, but its decision would not be "binding on all persons and parts of the government, henceforth ... [and would] not establish a 'supreme Law of the Land.'"[73] The concept may be debatable as sheer academic theory but pragmatically is at a major competitive disadvantage. Given Marshall's assertive and expansive chartings of judicial power, and the progressive extension of it since then, the theory probably is too belated to have any practical consequence. The momentum of Marshall's works have proved so inexorable that, despite episodes of dissatisfaction with how the judiciary exercises its authority, popular expectations would be breached if the Court were not supreme in both name and function.

# References

1. U.S. CONST., art. I, §9.
2. THE PAPERS OF THOMAS JEFFERSON 133 (J. Boyd ed. 1950).
3. *See* J. Locke, *An Essay Concerning the True Original, Extent and End of Civil Government* 3–143, in E. BARKER, SOCIAL CONTRACT (1980).
4. CONTINENTAL CONGRESS, DECLARATION AND RESOLVES (Oct. 14, 1774).
5. VIRGINIA DECLARATION OF RIGHTS para. 1 (Va. 1776).
6. Mass. Const. art. 1, *reprinted in* THE FOUNDERS' CONSTITUTION at 11 (P. Kurland & R. Lerner ed. 1987).
7. THE DECLARATION OF INDEPENDENCE, para. 1 (1776).
8. *Id.*
9. U.S. CONST., Preamble.
10. L. Levy, JUDICIAL REVIEW AND THE SUPREME COURT (1967).
11. *See* G. GUNTHER, CONSTITUTIONAL LAW 15 (1985).
12. *See id.*
13. *Id.*
14. *Id.*
15. 3 U.S. (Dall.) 386 (1798).
16. *See id.* at 398–400.
17. *See id.*
18. *Griswold v. Connecticut*, 381 U.S. 479, 510 (1965) (Black, J., dissenting).
19. *Id.* at 511–12 (Black, J., dissenting).
20. *Calder v. Bull*, 3 U.S. (Dall.) at 396–98.
21. *See id.*
22. *Griswold v. Connecticut*, 381 U.S. at 482.
23. *See, e.g., Lochner v. New York*, 198 U.S. 45, 56–57 (1905).
24. *See* U.S. CONST., amend. V.
25. 5 THE FOUNDERS CONSTITUTION, *supra* note 6, *quoting Bradshaw v. Rodgers*, 20 Johns R. 103 (N.Y. 1822).
26. *Id.*
27. *Id.*
28. *Id.* at 314, *quoting Bowman v. Middleton*, 1 Bay 252 (S.C. 1792).
29. *Fletcher v. Peck*, 10 U.S. (6 Cranch) 87, 139 (1810), *Scott v. Sanford*, 60 U.S. (19 How.) 393, 407 (1857).
30. *See* J. NOWAK, R. ROTUNDA, J. YOUNG, CONSTITUTIONAL LAW, § 11.1, at 333 (1986).
31. D. LLOYD, THE IDEA OF LAW 77 (1976).
32. U.S. CONST., amend. IX.
33. The nature and tone of the objections are concisely captured by Justice Black in *Griswold v. Connecticut*, 381 U.S. at 507–27 (Black, J., dissenting).
34. *See* L. Levy, *Supreme Court, 1789–1801*, AMERICAN CONSTITUTIONAL HISTORY 46 (Levy, Karst, Mahoney, ed.)
35. *See Marbury v. Madison*, 5 U.S. (1 Cranch) 137 (1803) (overturning Judiciary Act of 1789 in part and establishing power of judicial review).

36. *Id.*
37. *See* L. TRIBE, AMERICAN CONSTITUTIONAL LAW 861-62 (1988).
38. *See* R. McCLOSKEY, THE AMERICAN SUPREME COURT (1960).
39. Ideological screening of judicial nominees has been a common practice of administrations from Washington's to Reagan's. *See* H. ABRAHAM, JUSTICES AND PRESIDENTS (1974).
40. The Republican Congress, ushered in with Jefferson's inauguration, repealed the legislation expanding district and circuit courts and reducing the size of the Supreme Court. *See* I C. WARREN, THE SUPREME COURT IN UNITED STATES HISTORY 204-22 (1932).
41. *See Martin v. Hunter's Lessee,* 14 U.S. (1 Wheat.) 304 (1816).
42. Frankfurter, *John Marshall and the Judicial Function,* 69 HARV. L. REV. 217, 219 (1955).
43. *Marbury v. Madison,* 5 U.S. (1 Cranch) at 175.
44. *Marbury v. Madison,* 5 U.S. (1 Cranch) at 176-77.
45. *Id.*
46. U.S. CONST., art. III, §2.
47. *Marbury v. Madison,* 5 U.S. (1 Cranch) at 175-76.
48. *See Rescue Army v. Municipal Court of Los Angeles,* 331 U.S. 549, (1947), *citing,* Hayburn's Case, 2 Dall. 409 (1792).
49. *See* generally J. NOWAK, R. ROTUNDA, J. YOUNG, *supra* note 32, § 2.15 at 102-10.
50. *See Marbury v. Madison,* 5 U.S. (1 Cranch) at 166.
51. *See United States v. Nixon,* 418 U.S. 683, 704 (1974).
52. *Marbury v. Madison,* 5 U.S. (1 Cranch) at 177.
53. *Cooper v. Aaron,* 358 U.S. 1, 18 (1958).
54. 17 U.S. (4 Wheat.) 518 (1819).
55. U.S. CONST., Art. I, § 10.
56. *Dartmouth College v. Woodward,* 17 U.S. (4 Wheat.) at 628-50.
57. 17 U.S. (4 Wheat.) 316 (1819).
58. *Id.* at 418.
59. U.S. CONST., Art. I, § 8[3].
60. *McCulloch v. Maryland,* 17 U.S. (4 Wheat.) at 417.
61. *Id.*
62. *Id.* at 407-24.
63. *Id.* at 403-04.
64. *Id.* at 403-04.
65. 22 U.S. (9 Wheat.) 1 (1824).
66. *Id.* at 196.
67. *Id.* at 195-96.
68. *Lochner v. New York,* 198 U.S. 45 (1905).
69. *See Wickard v. Filburn,* 317 U.S. 111, 120 (1942).
70. *See Hodel v. Virginia Surface Mining & Reclamation Association, Inc.,* 452 U.S. 264 (1981) (upholding federal regulation of strip mining enacted pursuant to commerce clause); *Perez v. United States,* 402 U.S. 146 (1971) (upholding enactment, pursuant to commerce clause, making loan-sharking a federal crime); *Katzenbach v. McClung,* 379 U.S. 294 (1964); *Heart of Atlanta Motel, Inc. v. United States,* 379 U.S. 241 (1964)

(upholding federal civil rights legislation enacted pursuant to commerce clause).

71. *Cooper v. Aaron*, 358 U.S. at 18.
72. Meese III, *The Law of the Constitution*, 61, Tulane L. REV. 979, 983 (1987).
73. *Id.*

# Three

# The Case Against
# Judicial Activism

A central premise of representative governance is that the exercise of power must be tied to the consent of the governed.[1] President Lincoln, in his first inaugural address, asserted that if government policy is to be "made in ordinary litigation between parties in personal actions, the people will have ceased to be their own rulers."[2] Modern proponents of restraint sometimes use Lincoln's observation in arguing that the judiciary's function is "not to polic[e] or advis[e] Legislatures or Executives [but] . . . to decide the litigated case and to decide it in accordance with the law."[3] The circumstances in which that characterization of the judiciary's role emerged suggest a need for caution before investing in it.

Lincoln made the point at a time of enormous turmoil compounded by outrage over the Court's validation of slavery. Such an environment is not the ideal one for clear-headedness and articulation of principles for all seasons. Intimations that the judiciary is invariably antidemocratic unless properly cramped in its function, moreover, are exaggerated or misplaced. The assumption that judges are removed from the electoral process and thereby detached from the ultimate source of legitimacy disregards or discounts the manifold influences that ensure answerability to the citizenry. As discussed more comprehensively in Chapter Six, the judiciary is shaped by and responsive to democratic controls beginning with the appointment process and ending with the necessary

49

acceptability of its decisions to the rest of government and the public.

Contrary to the fears and anxieties of critics, the Court traditionally has been more attuned to majoritarian impulses and dominant preferences than not. None of its decisions has been more thoroughly condemned by history than the determination that blacks were "so far inferior ... that they ... might justly and lawfully be reduced to slavery."[4] Despite the morally underdeveloped nature of the holding and the rhetorical excoriation it evoked, the Court's racist sentiments probably were not far removed from the common sense of the time. Although critical of the proslavery decision, Lincoln himself recognized and catered to the virulent racism that permeated the citizenry's consciousness. In the course of his 1858 senatorial campaign, he proclaimed his belief in white supremacy and expressed objection to the possibility of citizenship for blacks.[5] Even what is arguably the Court's most contemptible decision thus was not without a sense for the public's pulse.

The argument that law-making should be an exclusive preserve of the legislature, because it is more directly accountable to the people, also does not accurately reflect political reality. The premise assumes a model of representation that does not exist now and ignores past manipulations and riggings of the electoral system in a fashion that often precluded idealized notions of accountability. A constitutional amendment extended the franchise to half of the citizenry only this century.[6] Although the right to vote is not constitutionally enumerated, the Court eventually recognized it as "a fundamental matter in a democratic society."[7] Only recently did it determine that schemes which discriminated against and denied citizens the opportunity to vote, or diluted the weight of their ballot, amounted to an equal protection violation.[8] Without judicial intervention to secure voting rights from poll taxes, literacy tests and other disabling devices, or insist upon reapportionment remedies that equalized voting power, theories of political accountability would be further deficient.

Even with remediation of discriminatory practices and malapportionment, assumptions that representatives are primarily accountable to their local constituents have been disrupted by the emergence and consequences of special interest groups whose concerns transcend a single electoral district.[9] Modern campaign financing and vote monitoring by political action committees create a competing accountability that may be even more critical to a representative's candidacy. Election or reelection thus may be more dependent upon a legislator's responsiveness to a political action group than to local voters. High incumbency rates testify both to the resource advantages of office and responsiveness to special interest groups. Legislative accountability is a fundamental expectation of and central assumption of many who depict the judiciary as antidemocratic. It has become increasingly susceptible, however, to charges of being mythical.

Accountability in theory or in practice is no assurance that responsibility will be exercised. The legislature at times even may rely upon the judiciary to conform its enactments to the demands of the constitution. Especially when legislators are transfixed by concern with adverse fallout from a potentially controversial action, hard decisions and consequent lawmaking responsibility sometimes pass to the judiciary by calculated default. A decade ago, the Court determined that Congress' prohibition of racial discrimination[10] in the creation and enforcement of contracts reached private as well as state parties.[11] A strong case exists that the holding, by reaching private transactions, surpassed original legislative contemplation. Even so, when the Court later considered reversing its determination, a majority of senators and substantial number of representatives urged that it not be done.[12] The Court subsequently reaffirmed that private contracts were within the purview of the statute in question.[13]

Critics maintain that legislative and presumably democratic consent cannot be inferred from a failure to enact a measure reasserting true and original intent. Justice Scalia has observed that policies perhaps too controversial to survive the legislative process can be more safely supported or opposed after being enshrined by a court decision.[14] He notes, moreover, that congressional failure to act may betoken any number of possibilities including

"(1) approval of the status quo as opposed to (2) inability to agree upon how to alter the status quo, (3) unawareness of the status quo; (4) indifference to the status quo, or even (5) political cowardice."[15] In the contract discrimination case, at least, the basis for congressional endorsement of the Court's original and arguably miscalculated judgment was not unclear. It rested upon concern that a "legislative effort to restore the interpretation would be fractious and divisive."[16] Even if the reasons for congressional inaction were more ambiguous, the basic problem would be less a matter of proper exercise of judicial power than of ultimate legislative responsibility. Insofar as the legislature has power to alter the reach and consequences of judicial review, any antidemocratic potential is a function of its own abdication.

Value-based inquiry, whether pursuant to legislative action or abnegation, is an essential dimension of judicial review. It has been argued that "The constitution's makers knew the need for change and provided for it" through the amendment process.[17] Constitutional provisions as noted earlier, however, were drafted in broad terms that obviously would require future inquiry and explication. The amendment process may afford a means for adding provisions desired by later generations or revising original prescriptions, but its cumbersome and difficult ways are not well suited for developing the document's meaning. Amendments that provide or guarantee rights are unlikely to be drafted in terms that eliminate the need for an infusion of values to animate them. The Fourteenth Amendment with its guarantees of due process and equal protection, for instance, continues to be a departure rather than ending point for establishing constitutional meaning.

The futility of relying upon the amendment process for establishing undisputed meaning is further shown by the proposed Equal Rights Amendment, which would have prohibited discrimination on the basis of sex. Typical of the constitution's broad enunciations, the eventual significance of such a passage would be shaped by the values that operated in adding necessary vitalizing principles to it. At the very outset, litigation invariably would arise over whether the guarantee permitted or precluded affirmative action policies establishing preferences on the basis of gender. Because the constitution is not always self-defining, and tends to be especially open-ended with respect to passages creating rights and liberties, reliance on the amendment process rather than judicial inquiry would impair rather than vitalize critical terms and provisions. Insofar as fundamental principles are dynamic as a consequence of the indefinite terms from which they emanate, flexible examination and expoundment guided by good faith effort to discern operative values are preferable to the less practicable and ultimately unserviceable task of formal constitutional revision.

Even many who recognize the need for and inevitability of value-based inquiry sometimes are uncomfortable with the discretion it affords the judiciary and thus endeavor to construct theoretical devices that would restrain its power to vitalize the constitution. Process restrictions generally provide no assurance against subjectivism, however, insofar as ideology may be purposely advanced under the guise of restraint. Even a conscious effort to adjudicate dispassionately is bound to reflect personal perspective, experience, limitations, bias and thus an unquantifiable measure of subjectivity. Concern that the judiciary is an antidemocratic institution nonetheless continues to fuel the notions that it must be subject to special process restraints.

Expressing a desire for inhibition has proved much easier than identifying a viable or tamper-proof analytical methodology. Theories of judicial review, urging strict construction of constitutional text, adherence to original intent or reliance upon neutral principles, share the motivating denominator of precluding or minimizing subjective decision-making. Although styled as means for enhancing the judiciary's claim to democratic legitimacy, they have the common denominator too of a utility that is illusory and potential for mischief that is significant.

Notions that the judiciary should perform an essentially mechanical task date back virtually to the institution's inception and have been restated and embellished upon often since. Justice Story described the constitution as "practical [in] nature, . . . designed for common use and fitted for common understanding."[18]

A century later, Justice Roberts observed that the Court need only "lay the article of the constitution which is involved beside the statute which is challenged and ... decide whether the latter squares with the former."[19] The inadequacy of strict constructionism as a constitutional methodology should have been recognized long ago. Controversy over whether the "necessary and proper" clause authorized Congress to enact only laws that were absolutely required and permitted by its specified powers, or to adopt unprohibited means useful in effectuating an allowable aim, presented an early profile in textual ambiguity and interpretive reality. Chief Justice Marshall's expansive definition of "necessary and proper" should have been a fatal blow to strict constructionism. Despite manifest deficiencies, however, it continues to have significant rhetorical value. It is the doctrinal antecedent too for some other harnessing concepts which, as discussed below, have proved to be no more compelling.

Theories of judicial restraint have been propounded under a variety of labels. Justice Black advanced perhaps the starkest version by insisting "the Court has no power to add to or subtract from the procedures set forth by the Founders."[20] Black maintained that the Court should read the constitution "in a straightforward manner, pay close attention to its words and avoid twisting or stretching [its] meanings, so there will be few occasions for controversies that can be manipulated."[21] He urged strict constructionism as a methodology to ensure results that would be objectively right rather than influenced by personal preference or ideology.

Insofar as the Court must make essentially mechanical decisions, such as whether a person who is not a citizen or resident of the United States or is under the age of thirty may serve as president or in the senate,[22] a simple textual focus is sufficient. Pure literalism has little if any utility, however, as a guide for reading such critical passages as "freedom of speech, ... of the press,"[23] "unreasonable searches,"[24] "speedy trial,"[25] "impartial jury,"[26] "Assistance of Counsel for his Defense,"[27] "Excessive bail,"[28] "cruel and unusual punishment,"[29] "privileges and immunities,"[30] "due process,"[31] and "equal protection."[32] The belief that such language reveals itself if only closely read, ignores the patent ambiguities necessitating a value-based inquiry and engraftment of principle so that the text will have meaning and relevance.

The Ninth and Tenth amendments, which reserve unspecified powers to the people[33] and the states,[34] are bereft of any specifics and were purposely created that way. A general promise of unenumerated rights and powers to the people and states respectively, as noted in chapter two, was designed to ensure that the Bill of Rights would not be regarded as an exclusive listing of fundamental guarantees and thus implicitly contemplated textual infusions. The presence of and reason for such open-ended residual provisions reinforces the notion that reference to extraconstitutional values and importation of principles is not only desirable but necessary if such passages are to have any meaning whatsoever.

The futility of strict literalism is further evidenced by the tortured mental gymnastics which must be resorted to on its behalf. Black consistently subscribed to the notion that the First Amendment's guarantees were unequivocal. Yet, his strict constructionist premise eventually failed as an analytical device for delineating the contours of freedom of expression. The term "speech" is not defined by the constitution and, because it can be read broadly to include symbolic expression or narrowly to include only verbal communication, eventually it required explication for which the constitution itself provided no guidance. The wearing of black armbands to protest the Vietnam War, for instance, was recognized by a majority of the Court as within the purview of speech.[35] Black would have regarded "standing, patrolling, or marching," even to make a political statement, as beyond the ambit of speech.[36] He likewise would have found the message "Fuck the Draft," emblazoned on a jacket and displayed in protest of government policy, to be unprotected conduct.[37]

By concluding that speech and conduct were conceptually and constitutionally separate, Black settled for a distinction that was more convenient than principled. His adoption of a more restrictive meaning of "speech" represented participation in active, competitive line-drawing. An exclusively textual focus thus failed even in the hands of perhaps its most prominent and ardent enthusiast.

Black's unbending adherence to strict constructionism reflected his sense that more flexible analytical methodologies weakened constitutional guarantees. If rights could be expanded, he observed, they also could be diluted.[38] The argument does not diminish the reality that much key constitutional language has no self-evident meaning and requires more than a dictionary reference. It is because literalism is such a patently insufficient interpretive guide that strict constructionists represent "a very unpopulated subgroup these days."[39] Urgings of such restraint nonetheless have been augmented by notions of originalism and neutrality,[40] which essentially would afford the judiciary a narrow band of latitude in enunciating constitutional law. If subscribed to, such concepts would weaken the judiciary and the constitution without meaningfully of curbing any potential for abuse.

Suggestions that the Court, when confronted with vague or indeterminate language, need only refer to the original intent of the framers are delusionary. Delegates to the Constitutional Convention, like the states which ratified the charter, may have supported the entire document or a given provision for diverse reasons. Identification of a singular intent at best is the product of guesswork, as even some prominent exponents of judicial restraint have acknowledged.[41] At worst, it invites self-serving mischief.

Constitutional guarantees may have been broadly supported in their framing and ratification, but reasons for that endorsement may have varied significantly. Advocates of the First Amendment's establishment clause, for instance, supported it for reasons that do not merge into a singular purpose. Its adoption reflected the coincidental confluence of at least three diverse interests which regarded the provision respectively as a safeguard against religious influence upon government, security against federal interference with established state religions and protection against official impediments to religious pluralism.[42] Emphasis upon the original intent of the establishment clause risks devolution into a search for the most serviceable purpose. Modern jurisprudence includes the contention that the establishment clause was adopted solely to prevent imposition of a state religion and possibly to deter sectarian discrimination.[43] Such an appraisal dismisses the concerns of those who regarded the provision as a means for creating a wall between church and state.[44] It also demonstrates how inquiries into original purpose are likely to reveal a selective rather than comprehensive reality.

Even if it were possible to discern the framers' intent, it would not necessarily follow that the identified purpose at the time of enactment or ratification should govern the present or future. Public education was an undeveloped and marginal social institution, for instance, when the Fourteenth Amendment was adopted.[45] Even in the North, strict racial segregation in or exclusion from public education was more common than not.[46] Many of the Fourteenth Amendment's architects considered liberty of contract to be a more critical key to equal protection and did not intend to prohibit formal segregation in schools or other venues.[47] Reference to original intent would be misplaced in a modern equal protection context, therefore, to the extent that it would disregard the altered dimensions and priorities of intervening teachings and subsequent circumstances. In eventually marking the demise of the separate but equal doctrine, the Court observed that "In these days, it is doubtful that any child may reasonably be expected to succeed in life if he is denied the opportunity of an education."[48] Constitutional inquiry and expoundment thus may require an accounting for and factoring in of altered perceptions, acquired knowledge and revised values.

Resistance to adaptive analysis effectively elevates the constitution's architects to a mythical status of omniscience and discounts the ability of subsequent generations to engage in a critical facet of self-governance. Jefferson's reference to the Constitutional Convention as an "assembly of demi–Gods" represents a flattering but hyperbolic characterization that is unfortunate insofar as it implies the framers were divinely inspired. In reality, they were professionals, farmers and merchants whose convergence upon Philadelphia in 1787 reflected a common sense that the union was foundering upon individual state jealousies and pettiness.[49] Their overarching aim was to construct a serviceable system of government that would avoid the pitfalls of the Articles of Confederation[50] and not pretend to contemplate every conceivable issue that might arise in the future. Such anticipation would have been beyond their capability anyway. Technological realities alone precluded even the remotest consideration of whether eavesdropping should be subject to the Fourth Amendment's reasonable search standards, or whether the electronic media should be part of the press and thereby protected by the First Amendment.

Apart from such obvious shortcomings of originalism, heavy emphasis upon framer's intent represents a disquieting preference for the judgment of the constitution's architects over their progeny. Subsequent generations have confronted and fought over the slavery issue and addressed realities never even contemplated by the drafters. As a consequence, the modern citizenry is the beneficiary of the accumulated wisdom from two centuries of constitutional experience. Exclusive or excessive reliance upon initial design represents investment in a manifestly imperfect rather than infallible assemblage. Unvarying subscription to early visions and perceptions disregards the reality that much valuable constitutional law has evolved from experience rather than original expectation. It also ignores that some precepts originally regarded as essential may seem less imperative now. The Third Amendment, for instance, owes its existence to the then freshly remembered and detested colonial experience of being forced to quarter British soldiers.[51] Even if a basic and uncontroverted notion, the Third Amendment since has receded into a largely functional anachronism.

Given a technologically sophisticated society with enormous intrusive capabilities, interests in personal privacy have evolved into a concern that is not explicitly protected by the constitution but is manifestly more profound now than the Third Amendment. Experience over two centuries, during which political and social realities have developed, thus has begotten new concepts of what is fundamental. Notions such as "privacy," "freedom of conscience," "freedom of the person," "freedom of choice of occupation" and "right to social welfare" are enumerated as basic guarantees in modern constitutions that borrow heavily from the vitalization, if not precise explications of, the American Constitution.[52] Excessive investment in framers' intent not only may reflect undue reverence for the constitution's architects but may impair animation of a document with relevance that is both immediate and enduring.

The overt failings or limitations of literalism and originalism have helped to beget a more complex model of analysis that also claims security against subjectivism. The neutral principles theory of review purports that "Where constitutional materials do not clearly specify the value to be preferred, there is no principled way to prefer any claimed human value to any other . . ., [so a] judge must stick close to the text and the history, and their fair implications, and not construct new rights."[53] The concept of neutrality translates into a license to import values qualified by insistence that consequent principles be applied with objective constancy. A court's obligation, pursuant to that analytical formula, is to devise general principles that favor no particular interest and apply them consistently even if later results might be subjectively distasteful.

Neutrality, like literalism and originalism, is better consigned to theory than practice. A court that found discrimination unconstitutional because race should be irrelevant, for instance, might consider itself bound to find affirmative action unconstitutional pursuant to the same predicate and thus reach a consistent result. Supposedly neutral principles are sufficiently malleable, however, so that a court could reach a contrary but principled decision. An equally neutral premise, making race irrelevant except for redressing past discrimination, could support findings that discrimination generally was unconstitutional but permissible if tied to remediation. The coursing of affirmative action jurisprudence effectively demonstrates the disutility of neutral principles when they would seem most desired.

Some members of the Court regard color-conscious remedies as being generically less invidious than traditional classifications discriminating on the basis of race and thus are inclined to reconcile them with the guarantee of equal protection.[54] Others are disposed toward characterizing any racial classification, whether designed to remediate or overtly exclusionary, as constitutionally noxious.[55] The doctrinal schism, reflecting disagreement upon and competition of values in defining the extent to which equal protection requires color-blindness, demonstrates that divergent results may be reached from the same starting point. It also shows that when a value is identified, such as color-blindness, and is engrafted upon the constitution, as in vitalizing the equal protection guarantee, neutrality fails to afford any objective steerage or stopping point for the principle's operation.

The neutrality formula at its worst may encourage blind adherence to precedent. Such analysis does no service to the quality of constitutional law, which may require adaptation to social gyrations or inverted conditions. In demanding school desegregation in the face of massive southern resistance, for instance, the Court concluded that neighborhood school and freedom of choice plans did not satisfy equal protection demands for a unitary school system.[56] Residential migration and settlement patterns rather than official defiance and obstruction of a desegregation order, however, is now more pertinent to the interest of racially mixed schools. As a consequence, plans that previously were forbidden because they subverted equal protection aims now may be desirable because they facilitate them. What were previously unconstitutional means in fact are now being advanced as methodologies that may promote constitutional ends by deterring resegregation. A neutrality standard, that might impair a court's ability to consider whether a previously intolerable concept could facilitate contemporary interests in integration maintenance, would be a major disservice to the interest of constitutional relevance.

Although a principle may be embraced in one instance, enduring adherence to it may be a reflection of fossilized rather than enlightened thought. Insistence upon congruency of results in purportedly similar instances disregards inevitable disagreement over what facts and issues are genuinely alike. The neutral principles model is further flawed insofar as it presumes that a singular principle links multifold decisions into a coherent body of law. Constitutional rulings tend to be based upon multiple principles, rather than any single unifying one, and the relative emphasis upon those precepts may vary. The Court, for instance, originally held that a shopping center was the functional equivalent of a company town and thus peaceful labor picketing there could not be enjoined.[57] Although it appeared that the nature of the forum was the determinative concern in that instance, another principle — the nature of the expression — was pivotal in a subsequent but practically indistinguishable case. In the later instance, the Court upheld an injunction against antiwar leafleting at a shopping center, because the expression did not relate to the site's activities.[58] To the extent decisions rest upon multiple principles, therefore, neutrality is no assurance against varying or conflicting results begotten by a subjective shift in emphasis or tone.

What might otherwise appear to be a deviation from an original premise also may follow from the evolution of principles, neither formulated nor foreseen, from the time that precedent was set. The determination that automobiles could be searched without a warrant was originally tied to vehicular mobility.[59] Later, in justifying warrantless searches even if an automobile had been officially immobilized and secured, the Court observed that individuals have a diminished expectation of privacy in a motor vehicle.[60] A warrant to search would have been required in the subsequent case if the initial concern with mobility had governed. Because enunciation of a neutral principle does not preclude amplification or augmentation, it also does not bar revisionism, creativity or obfuscation. Nor ultimately does neutrality preclude the subjectivism, begotten by conscience, convenience or unawareness, against which it supposedly operates.

Theories of judicial restraint tend to be as unimpressive as their implementation would be mischief laden. Judicial reticence may ensure that inquiry terminates where it should commence. The notion that a judge can discover the meaning of and properly apply the constitution, if text, history and structure are closely scrutinized or principles are consistent, ignores the nature of the document and diminishes the institution responsible for activating it. Because text, history and structure often are equivocal or uncertain, and are especially so at the constitution's most crucial points, importation and development of values from outside the charter's four corners sometimes is essential.

Reference to external value as a preface to engrafting principle is not a drastic notion, if the constitution's reservation of unenumerated liberties and rights[61] and broad articulation of liberty, equal protection and other fundamental guarantees are to be sensed logically. Although purportedly tied to constitutional text and structure,[62] modern rights of privacy are better understood as an engraftment of principle flowing from external values. Despite linking the right of privacy to the purported emanations of six express constitutional guarantees,[63] critics were correct in declaring they could not find it "in the Bill of Rights [or] in any other part of the constitution."[64] Whether presented as a constitutional emanation, penumbra or implication, any such principle not expressly enumerated by the constitution derives from external values and is glossed upon it. Given the document's natural law ancestry and the invitation of and responsibility for its open-ended terms, objections to that grafting process stake out a position that is both radical and untenable.

Despite protestations over the introduction of external values, advertence to them is so established that it often escapes notice. Extrinsic inquiry is responsible for the general determination, for instance, that equal protection is concerned with official classification of some persons but not others. In originally interpreting the equal protection clause, the Court "doubt[ed] very much whether any action of a state not directed by way of discrimination against . . . negroes as a class, or on account of their race, will ever be held to come within the purview of this provision."[65] A century later, however, discrimination on grounds of gender, alienage and parentage had come within the ambit of equal protection. Although originally uncontemplated, solicitude for discrimination on grounds other than race emerged pursuant to an externally referenced conclusion that "prejudice against [any] discrete and insular minority may create a special condition."[66]

Because government regularly classifies when it enacts legislation,[67] such constitutional engraftment is essential for creating limiting principles that prevent a progressive tax system, government benefits scheme and other relativities from being swallowed by equal protection. If it is assumed that equal protection means something less than absolute equality in all instances and more than nothing, constitutional lines must be etched with reference to some scheme of values that is independent of the constitution. Even if couched in terms of extrapolation or implication, such determinations represent pronouncements of what the constitution should be rather than what it demonstrably is.

Controversy over and dissatisfaction with the exercise of responsibility are the inevitable wages of any decision-making institution. For each complaint that the judiciary functions antidemocratically, substantial evidence exists of an institutional predilection toward majoritarian preferences. Some of its constitutional expoundments thus have been cited as evidence that the Court suffers from an "acute ethnocentric myopia" diminishing its sensitivity toward the nation's pluralistic fabric.[68] Judicial pronouncements on race, religion, lifestyle and expression, when taken as a whole and examined dispassionately, are less vulnerable to criticism for disregarding popular will than for an "inability to appreciate that in our land of cultural pluralism, there are many who think, act, and talk differently from the members of [the] Court."[69] Constitutional text itself provides more opportunities for engraftment of principle than the Court actually has accepted. The Ninth Amendment's undeveloped state is an especially prominent reminder of how reticent the Court has been in fashioning a constitutional landscape inhospitable to majoritarian interests. Given the Ninth Amendment's history and nature, retreat from its implications actually may be regarded as an extreme variant of restraint.[70] Insofar as it reflects worries about the antimajoritarian potential of the provision and subjectivity of its amplification, circumspection is a function of sensitivity to perceived democratic imperatives. At the same time, such review or lack thereof is driven no less by reference to external values and concerns than analysis which sought to vitalize the Ninth Amendment's or any other open-ended provision's meaning.

The deleterious consequences of judicial inaction militate, even at the risk of subjectivism, in favor of seeking to discern, develop and even add to fundamental rights. Identification of the values which such principles are premised upon may be a treacherous process, as evinced by the Court's persistent emphasis on economic freedom during the first third of this century. As discussed in Chapter Five, the Court's tenacious defense of marketplace freedom gave value-based inquiry and constitutional engraftment a bad name that still endures.

Since the constitutional demise of economic rights, the Court has endeavored to control its inquiry into values by considering whether a concept is "implicit in a scheme of ordered liberty" or rooted in the "traditions and conscience of our people."[71] Such formulations on their face purport to tie any enunciation of principle to values that at least arguably are suggested by the constitution or anchored in its foundation. As critics of the right to privacy have noted, however, such verbal formulas may ensure only that personal ideology is presented in constitutional wrapping for ritualistic rather than substantive purposes. No standard purporting to control process is immune to subjectivism. Even the now discredited notion of economic liberty legitimately and scrupulously might be advocated as within the possible ambit of either standard.

The ultimate linkage of the constitutional grafting process to democratic expectations flows from a conscientious effort to discern values and formulate principles which can be widely embraced. Review in practice either immediately or inexorably has accommodated principle to dominant preference rather than force-fed unpopular values over an extended period of time. Sensitivity not just to process but result, by its respective absence and presence, has accounted for the functioning[72] and foiling[73] of involuntary sterilization programs. From recognition that marriage

and procreation were interests that deserved parity with constitutionally explicated guarantees emerged what eventually was
configured as the right of privacy.[74] In the process, the Court
demonstrated a needless fixation with the image that it was unlock-
ing meaning hidden within the document itself. Mooring the right
of privacy to purported constitutional emanations spoke more to
the judiciary's preoccupation with the appearance that it was
deciphering the constitution's mysteries than with an honest portrayal of its responsibility to discern values and engraft needed
principle.

Arguments may be framed over how broadly the Court has
stretched privacy rights, as the abortion controversy demonstrates,
or delimited them, as the refusal to include homosexuality within
its scope evinces.[75] It would be a sterile philosophy of governance,
alien to the values of personal worth, independence and dignity
proclaimed in the society's founding and reiterated since, that would
disable the judiciary from recognizing interests "fundamental to the
very existence and survival of the race" and protective of individual
intimacy and autonomy. A process that identifies values perceived
to be relevant and significant, and from them constructs principles
of a fundamental nature, does not necessarily demean the constitution or contravene democratic principles. Pretending that such
review represents the constitution speaking rather than the
judiciary making it speak is less than candid and even deceitful. At
the same time, projection of a sense that constitutional meaning is
unfolding from within the document rather than being affixed to
it reveals a judiciary deeply concerned with democratic imperatives.
What eventually must be appreciated both by the Court and its
detractors is that constitutional embellishment referenced to external values is legitimate, so long as the reason for it is convincing and
the citizenry immediately or eventually subscribes to it.

If externally referenced constitutional law is objected to on
grounds it poses unacceptable risks to a democratic system, it is fair
to consider the consequences in the absence of such enhancement.
The legacy of judicial inaction, in the face of serious affront by federal
or state government, is not an estimable one. In addition to forced

sterilization, the record of judicial quiescence and resultant constitutional torpor includes incarceration of political dissenters,[76] coerced relocation and dispossession of citizens declared a threat to national security,[77] McCarthyism[78] and segregation.[79] Because a veneer of deference is capable of masking result-oriented analysis, professions of restraint may facilitate the worst of both worlds.

In championing the notion of economic freedom, for instance, the Court professed not to be second-guessing legislative judgment.[80] It confessed in the next breath, however, that it objected to "the soundness of the views which uphold this law."[81] Racist ideology cloaked in the trappings of deference, as a further example, accounted for the Court's proslavery decisions before the Civil War. Despite subsequent modifications of the constitution and crafting of federal law designed to secure equality of citizenship and rights,[82] the Court in the lexicon of restraint reinvested in the ideology of racial supremacy and continued to function as the guardian of constitutional inequality. As a consequence, equal protection review for half of the Fourteenth Amendment's existence reinforced rather than dismantled official segregation.

The separate but equal doctrine formally constitutionalized a system that in theory and practice was calibrated to promote separateness rather than equality. Even when first articulated, in *Plessy v. Ferguson*,[83] the principle was criticized as a device for promoting objectives at odds with the constitution. By observing that official racial classifications were justified by community custom and tradition and public interest in peace, comfort and order, the Court expressed its own sense that separation was in society's best interest.[84]

Professions of deference to established ways revealed a variant of restraint that also borrowed from outside values and introduced them to the constitution. Justice Harlan, in dissent, observed that the formula was an affirmative means for protecting the advantages of a dominant class at the expense of a minority.[85] Even Harlan, however, was moved to comment that he had no doubt of the white race's superiority. Soon thereafter, he authored an opinion revealing further the invidious motivation and nature of the separate but equal doctrine.

When the Court unanimously upheld the closure of a black high school, while a white high school continued to operate,[86] it was apparent that the only relevant component of the separate but equal doctrine was its first half. The Court thus commenced a lengthy subscription to the notion that the Fourteenth Amendment "could not have been intended to abolish distinctions based upon color, or to enforce social, as distinguished from political equality, or a commingling of the two races upon terms unsatisfactory to either."[87]

Given the manifestly racist nature of the separate but equal doctrine, it is not surprising that official policy accentuated separation at the expense of equality. Consistent with the Court's own ideology, black education could be funded at a fraction of the amount afforded white education.[88] Constitutional doctrine thus proved immediately notable as a methodology accommodating separation to the point equality not only might be slighted but rendered entirely illusory.[89] Overt and pervasive discriminatory practices thus became the norm rather than the exception, given the Court's conviction that such ways responded to distinctions "in the nature of things."[90] Vestiges of that official legacy persist even now, as discriminatory legislation from that era still is being challenged and invalidated.[91] Antimiscegenation laws and other devices intended to maintain white purity and superiority persisted until just a couple of decades ago.[92]

Professions of deference thus merely sheathed an energy force responsible for a society that was partitioned by law and remained functionally divided even beyond the separate but equal doctrine's termination. By catering to dominant conventions and expectations, the Court could claim democratic legitimacy even if not the enduring sanction of morality. Nor would a contrary decision necessarily have sacrificed the latter for the former. The Court's obligation, if it had declared segregation unlawful, would have been to present a convincing justification for its constitutionally driven social engineering. It eventually performed that function half a century later when, despite substantial resistance, the Court's conclusions and reasoning proved persuasive enough at least eventually to be generally embraced though later qualified. Failure to disapprove segregation prior to then denotes again an institution closely wired to majoritarian rather than pluralistic concerns.

More than half a century's worth of constitutional law cast in deferential terms, but assuming racial superiority and rationalizing inequality and injustice, is a poor testament to restraint as a safeguard against the dangers of subjectivism. As the separate but equal doctrine's operation helps demonstrate, outside values will shape constitutional law regardless of how the judicial function is characterized. Proponents of restraint nonetheless suggest that a judiciary which overtly references constitutional law to external values is exclusively synonymous with one that breaches democratic principles.

History has demonstrated, given the Court's past enunciation of the separate but equal doctrine and articulation of economic rights, that professions of restraint may hide review that incontrovertibly is outcome-oriented. It follows that criticism too can present concerns couched in terms of process but more genuinely related to convenience of result. Selective criticism of the pertinent methodology thus counsels that the source and not just the nature of the rebuke should be examined. The Reagan Administration, for instance, consistently denounced the Court's privacy decisions on grounds they "creat[e] rights out of whole cloth that are not in the constitution."[93] Behind the condemnation, however, appeared to lurk a more material concern with inconvenience of result. Operative too was what seemed to be a sophisticated understanding of how professions of restraint can be effective camouflage for cynical advancement of political aims through the judiciary.

Despite a declared opposition to judge-made law,[94] Reagan ran for the presidency pursuant to the promise of appointing "at all levels of the judiciary [those] who respect family values and the sanctity of innocent human life."[95] The operation of family values in the construction of law is not mandated by the constitution. As an undeniably external reference point, therefore, family values also cut cloth that may be stitched to the constitution but is not of the charter's own spinning. Definition of the interest itself is as subjective as the results it is capable of begetting. Family values have the potential, depending upon their underlying meaning, to lead toward unanticipated and conflicting results. That capability is demonstrated by judicial intervention to protect of extended families from encumbering regulation.[96]

Importation of family values to embellish the meaning of liberty, so that it protected such households from having to abandon or alter their lifestyle, has been criticized for creating a new right "at will."[97] The objection, therefore, speaks to priorities and results rather than general principle. It is difficult to take seriously a philosophy that refers to family values as a basis for narrowing or eliminating abortion rights but abruptly cuts short their relevance elsewhere. Such a concept of review, no matter how elegantly stated, represents primarily a framework for intellectual and political hypocrisy.

Political rhetoric notwithstanding, Reagan's record shows a determination to appoint judges who were ideologically sympathetic toward his agenda.[98] Neither the commitment nor the hypocrisy is novel. President Roosevelt had a similar interest when, during the 1930s, he stressed the urgency of saving the constitution from the Court, and the Court from itself, but at bottom was concerned primarily with a judicial demeanor more hospitable to his New Deal policies.[99]

The Reagan Administration deserves credit for retooling and refining the appointment process, however, so that performance might be predicted more accurately and the possibility of ideological deviation minimized. The advent of computer technology and its usage in tracing prospective nominees' personal and professional backgrounds,[100] plus Reagan's experience with the unexpected performance of a justice he appointed to the state supreme court while governor of California,[101] merged toward creation of more fail-safe screening devices. The consequent disparity between philosophical profession and pronounced ideological and result oriented designs reveals further the deceiving and unprincipled nature of much contemporary criticism. From that self-contradiction emerges the dominant reality that objections to externally referenced constitutional law often reflect merely an altered set of priorities.

Because the constitution does not speak for itself, no theory of review has a claim to, much less a monopoly upon, any innate energizing force or wisdom. The quality of debate and review, not to mention common understanding, would benefit by more accurate representations of constitutional ways and means. Instead of facilitating the image that constitutional law flows forth from the document itself, aided only by judicial incantation or sage discernment of text, structure or spirit, the Court and its critics would serve the public better by more honestly portraying the process. Democratic interests stand to prosper rather than suffer from a confession that the constitution does not announce its bidding, and the consequent embellishments that actuate it are dependent upon the citizenry's ultimate embrace of or abidance by them.

# References

1. *See, e.g.,* A BICKEL, THE LEAST DANGEROUS BRANCH 16–20 (1962).
2. First Inaugural Address (Mar. 4, 1861).
3. Wechsler, *Toward Neutral Principles of Constitutional Law,* 73 HARV. L.REV. 1, 6 (1959).
4. *Scott v. Sanford,* 60 U.S. (19 How.), 393, 407 (1857).
5. R. DEVINE, T. BREEN, G. FREDRICKSON, R. WILLIAMS, AMERICA PAST AND PRESENT 405 (1984).
6. By constitutional amendment, women were given the right to vote in 1920. U.S. CONST., am. XIX. The Voting Rights Act of 1965, 42 U.S.C. §1973, was necessary to eliminate official barriers to voting by black citizens and thus secure the franchise for them.
7. *Reynolds v. Sims,* 377 U.S. 533, 554–55 (1964).
8. *See id.; Harper v. Virginia Board of Education,* 383 U.S. 663 (1966) (invalidating poll tax).
9. *See Garcia v. San Antonio Metropolitan Transit Authority,* 469 U.S. 528, 584 (1985) (O'Connor, J., concurring).
10. 42 U.S.C. § 1981.
11. *Runyon v. McCrary,* 427 U.S. 160 (1976).
12. *See* Reidinger, *Runyon* under the Gun, 78 A.B.A.J. 78, 80 (Nov. 1, 1988).
13. *Patterson v. McLean Credit Union,* 109 S.Ct. 2363, 2371–72 (1989). Although

acknowledging that 42 U.S.C. § 1981 prohibited discrimination in making and enforcing contracts, the Court nonetheless narrowed its scope so it does not reach post-formation harassment. *Id.* at 2373-74.

14. *See Johnson v. Transportation Agency, Santa Clara County*, 480 U.S. 616, 671 (1987).

15. *Id.* at 672.

16. *See* Reidinger, *supra* note 12, at 80.

17. *Griswold v. Connecticut*, 381 U.S. 479, 522 (Black, J., dissenting).

18. 1 J. STORY, COMMENTARIES ON THE CONSTITUTION OF THE UNITED STATES 345 (1905).

19. *United States v. Butler*, 297 U.S. 1, 62 (1935).

20. *See, e.g., In re* Winship, 397 U.S. 358, 377 (1970) (Black, J., dissenting).

21. L. TRIBE, AMERICAN CONSTITUTIONAL LAW, § 2-1, at 41 (1978).

22. Such eligibility standards for the presidency and senate are set respectively by U.S. CONST., art. II, §5 and art. I., §3.

23. U.S. CONST., amend. I.

24. *Id.*, amend. IV.

25. *Id.*, amend. VI.

26. *Id.*

27. *Id.*

28. *Id.*, amend. VIII.

29. *Id.*

30. *Id.*, amend. XIV, §1.

31. *Id.*

32. *Id.*

33. *Id.*, amend IX.

34. Id., amend. X.

35. *See Tinker v. Des Moines Independent School Dist.*, 393 U.S. 503, 505-06 (1969).

36. *Cox v. Louisiana*, 379 U.S. 559, 581 (1965) (Black, J., concurring).

37. *Cohen v. California*, 403 U.S. 15, 27 (1971) (Black, J., dissenting).

38. *See Griswold v. Connecticut*, 381 U.S. at 509 (Black, J., dissenting).

39. G. Gunther, Constitutional Law 529 n. 10 (1985).

40. Detailed accounts of the theories are set forth in A. BICKEL, THE LEAST DANGEROUS BRANCH (1962); L. HAND, THE BILL OF RIGHTS (1958); Bork, *Neutral Principles and Some First Amendment Problems*, 47 IND. L.J. 1 (1971); Weschler, *supra* note 3. For critical responses, *see, e.g.*, Tushnet, *Following the Rules Laid Down: A Critique of Interpretivism and Neutral Principles*, 96 HARV. L. REV. 781 (1983); Deutsch, *Neutrality, Legitimacy, and the Supreme Court: Some Intersections Between Law and Political Science*, 20 STAN L. REV. 169 (1968); Wright, *The Role of the Supreme Court in a Democratic Society. Judicial Activism or Restraint?* 54 CORN. L. REV. 1, (1968).

41. *See, e.g., Edwards v. Aguillard*, 107 S.Ct. 2573, 2605 (1987) (Scalia, J., dissenting); *Trimble v. Gordon*, 430 U.S. 762, 782-83 (1977) (Rehnquist, J., dissenting) (quoting *Village of Arlington Heights v. Metropolitan Housing Dev. Corp.*, 429 U.S. 252, 265 (1977).

42. *See* Van Alstyne, Trends in the Supreme Court: Mr. Jefferson's Crumbling Wall, 1984 DUKE L.J. 770, 773-74.

43. *See Wallace v. Jaffree*, 472 U.S. 38, 92 (Rehnquist, J., dissenting).

44. *See* Van Alstyne, *supra* note 42, at 776–79.

45. *See Brown v. Board of Education*, 347 U.S. 483, 490 (1954).

46. *See* L. TRIBE, GOD SAVE THIS HONORABLE COURT 46 (1985).

47. *See id.*

48. *Brown v. Board of Education*, 347 U.S. at 493.

49. R. DEVINE, *et al.*, *supra* note 5, at 168.

50. *See H. P. Hood, & Sons v. DuMond*, 336 U.S. 525, 533–34 (1949).

51. The Third Amendment provides that "(n)o soldier shall, in time of peace be quartered in any house, without the consent of the Owner, nor in time of war, but in a manner to be prescribed by law." U.S. CONST. am. III.

52. The proposed Basic Law of Hong Kong, for instance, enumerates these and other fundamental guarantees. *See* Draft Basic Law of the Hong Kong Special Administration Region of the People's Republic of China, Ch. 3, art. 27, 29, 31, 32 and 35.

53. Bork, *supra* note 40, at 8.

54. *See, e.g., City of Richmond v. J.A. Croson Company*, 109 S.Ct. 706, 752 (1989) (Marshall, J., dissenting).

55. *See id.* at 721.

56. *See, e.g., Green v. County School Board*, 391 U.S. 430, 441–42 (1968) ("freedom of choice" plan could not effectuate transition to unitary system); *Griffin v. County School*, 377 U.S. 218, 234 (1964) (closing of public schools for which desegregation ordered while at same time increasing funding for white children at private schools denied black children equal protection); *Goss v. Board of Educ.*, 373 U.S. 683, 685–87 (1963) (striking down transfer systems because such systems perpetuate segregation).

57. *Amalgamated Food Employees Local 590 v. Logan Valley Plaza*, 391 U.S. 308, 319 (1968), *overruled by Hudgens v. N.L.R.B.*, 424 U.S. 507 (1976).

58. *Lloyd Corp. v. Tanner*, 407 U.S. 551, 564 (1972). The Court eventually determined that speech content was an irrelevant concern and concluded that privately owned shopping centers were not so alike company towns that the state action doctrine should operate. *Hudgens v. N.L.R.B.*, 424 U.S. 507 (1976).

59. *Carroll v. United States*, 267 U.S. 132 (1925), *overruled by Chambers v. Maroney*, 399 U.S. 42 (1970). The basic concern, given probable cause that the motor vehicle contained contraband, was that it readily could be moved out of the jurisdiction and evidence would be lost. *Carrol*, 267 U.S. at 153.

60. *United States v. Chadwick*, 433 U.S. 1 (1977). By focusing upon a diminished expectation of privacy, rather than exigent circumstances, the Court was able to justify a warrantless search regardless of whether the vehicle might later be moved. *Id.* at 12–13.

61. *See* Chapter Two.

62. *See Griswold v. Connecticut*, 381 U.S. at 484–85, (right of privacy emanates from core guarantees in Bill of Rights).

63. *See id.*

64. *Id.* at 530 (Stewart, J., dissenting).

65. Slaughter-House Cases, 83 U.S. (16 Wall.), 36, 81 (1873).

66. *San Antonio Independent School District v. Rodriguez*, 411 U.S. 1, 28 (1973).

67. *See generally, Washington Davis*, 426 U.S. 229, 248 (1976).

68. *FCC v. Pacifica Foundation*, 438 U.S. 726, 775–76 (1978) (Brennan, J., dissenting).

69. *Id.*

70. Grey, Do We Have an Unwritten Constitution? 27 STAN. L.REV. 703, 716 (1975).

71. *E.g., Bowers v. Hardwick*, 478 U.S. 186, 191–92 (1986); *Roe v. Wade*, 410 U.S. 113, 152 (1973).

72. *See Buck v. Bell*, 274 U.S. 200 (1927).

73. *See Skinner v. Oklahoma*, 316 U.S. 1110 (1942).

74. *See Griswold v. Connecticut*, 381 U.S. at 484.

75. *See Bowers v. Harwick*, 478 U.S. 186 (1986).

76. Eugene Debs, who as the Socialist Party presidential candidate in 1920 attracted approximately 9 million votes, spent the campaign in prison for criticizing American participation in World War I. It has been noted that Debs' incarceration was comparable to having incarcerated Democratic presidential candidate George McGovern for his criticism of the Vietnam War during the 1972 campaign. *See* Kalven, *Ernst Freund and the First Amendment Tradition*, 40 U. Chi. L.Rev. 235, 237 (1973).

77. *See Korematsu v. United States*, 323 U.S. 214 (1944).

78. For a succinct summary of the Court's deference and unresponsiveness to McCarthyism, *see* J. NOWAK, R. ROTUNDA & J. YOUNG, CONSTITUTIONAL LAW §16.14, at 859–62 (1986).

79. *See Plessy v. Ferguson*, 163 U.S. 537 (1896).

80. *Lochner v. New York*, 198 U.S. 45, 56–57 (1905).

81. *Id.* at 61.

82. The Thirteenth, Fourteenth and Fifteenth amendments, and Civil Rights Acts of 1866 and 1870 all were designed, essentially to establish and effectuate the rights and equality of former slaves.

83. 163 U.S. 537 (1896).

84. *See id.* at 551.

85. *Id.* at 560–62 (Harlan, J., dissenting).

86. *Cumming v. Richmond County Board of Education*, 175 U.S. 528 (1899).

87. *Plessy v. Ferguson*, 163 U.S. at 544.

88. South Carolina in 1915, for instance, spent almost ten times more money per white student then black student. *See* A. LEWIS, PORTRAIT OF A DECADE: THE SECOND AMERICAN REVOLUTION 20 (1964).

89. *See Cumming v. Richmond County Board of Education*, 175 U.S. at 544.

90. *Plessy v. Ferguson*, 163 U.S. at 544.

91. *Hunter v. Underwood*, 471 U.S. 222 (1985) (invalidating voter disfranchisement statute expressly adopted in 1901 to deny blacks right to vote).

92. *See, e.g., Loving v. Virginia*, 388 U.S. 1 (1967).

93. Brownstein, *With or Without Supreme Court Changes, Reagan Will Reshape the Federal Bench*, 49 NAT'L J. 2338, 2341 (1984).

94. *Id.* at 2340.

95. *Id.*

96. *See Moore v. City of East Cleveland*, 431 U.S. 494 (1977).

97. *Moore v. City of East Cleveland*, 431 U.S. at 506 (White, J., dissenting).

98. *See* Brownstein, *supra* note 93, at 2340.

99. *See infra* Chapter Five.

100. *See* Goldman, *Reorganizing The Judiciary: The First Term Appointments*, 68 JUDICATURE 313, 315 (1985).

101. *See Reagan's Full Court Press*, NEW REPUBLIC, June 10, 1985, at 16, 18.

# Four

# The Self-Containing Ways of Activism

Characterization of the judiciary as an antidemocratic institution is mystifying insofar as its performance repeatedly has demonstrated how attuned and responsive the Court is to majoritarian preferences. Criticism of law woven from nontextual cloth fails to make some key distinctions regarding how the judiciary exercises its power and what accounts for principles that are legitimate and enduring. The democratic consonance of documental embellishment cannot be gauged simply by assessing whether resultant principles displace or uphold conventional wisdom. The judiciary's support for official segregation is a notable example of externally-referenced lawmaking that affirmed legislative judgment but begot a foul heritage.

Desegregation, the right to privacy and expansive contouring of First Amendment freedoms comprise a more positive legacy for a process that derives principle from outside values. The contrasting quality and durability of judgments are explainable not on grounds some were externally referenced but others were not. What the disparate results collectively demonstrate is that quality of outcome and reasoning is a passkey to democratic legitimacy. Public acclaim hinges not on technicality of process, or criteria that focus on interpretive myth rather than reality, but persuasive argument that convinces the citizenry of a value's pertinence and principle's validity.

# Judicial Review

It is not uncommon for fissures to develop between constitutional ideals and society's actual ways. Freedom of speech is easy to endorse as a general principle, for instance, but sometimes difficult to countenance when expressive content is personally objectionable or discomforting. Judgment that capitulates to political or societal distortion, or disclaims any responsibility for preventing it, may trade profits of short-term popularity for long-term esteem. Deference to the ugly impulses of the McCarthy era explains why decisions upholding the imprisonment of political dissenters at that time represent a low point in First Amendment history. Especially at such moments, when a noticeable cleavage exists between societal norms and events, decisions cutting against popular inclinations should not reflexively be equated with an antidemocratic function.

Judicial review that is candid in its identification and explanation of principle and works to advance a compelling reason for it may beget dispute, but it is less likely to breed disrepute. The opposite tends to be true when the Court is too timorous for the circumstances or, at the other pole, overconfident of its wisdom to the point that it assumes answers more readily than it raises questions and makes no meaningful effort to demonstrate that its conclusions are supported by compelling reasons.

The ultimate acceptability of judicially crafted standards and demands depends largely upon whether purpose and result are clearly and persuasively connected to values that are or can be widely acclaimed. Identification and delineation of basic guarantees, even if unenumerated, should not be worrisome insofar as the judiciary recognizes and satisfies the need to explain forthrightly and convincingly its choice of values and reasons for its conclusion. The Court's decisions may be unpopular or unwelcome and transcend constitutional text and even common understanding or expectation. Such eventualities and the process begetting them need not be troublesome, however, insofar as a fair-minded citizenry finds the underlying rationale persuasive and the result is perceived as right. Fair-mindedness, as Southern resistance to desegregation evidenced, may not be immediately present. Democratic interests are not necessarily subverted, however, when judicial review overrides popular instinct. The test of whether a constitutional embellishment has the consent of the governed must not be measured by popular response within the first days or even years after the relevant judgment. Proper assessment may require the passage of time for persuasion to overcome prejudice and uninformedness or for the principle itself to be fine-tuned or recalibrated. In either event, it is difficult to imagine any principle becoming a constitutional fixture without eventual broad support or at least countenance.

Many of the Court's constitutional engraftments, condemned sometimes as intemperate and unrooted in the document itself, are the product of evolutionary rather than revolutionary thought. The right of privacy has been ritually criticized, for instance, as the end point of an unauthorized flight of judicial fancy.[1] Contrary to rhetorical assaults upon the concept, the right relates back nearly a century to Louis Brandeis' seminal exposition on the subject.[2] The eventual emergence of the right of privacy as a constitutionally protected interest exemplifies how, when the Court conscientiously and openly strives to identify and effectuate fundamental values, pertinent truths about and expectations of society may be discerned and facilitated.

The relatively recent recognition that marriage and procreation are fundamental interests, even if not constitutionally enumerated, was not a radical or dogmatic pronouncement. A conclusion that those activities were essential to human "existence and survival,"[3] may seem to be an obviously merited effectuation of values near and dear to society. It would be an impermissible result, however, if review were limited only to principles extractable from the constitution itself.

A strong argument may be composed that recognition of the right to privacy was more belated than misconceived. A decade before the seeds for privacy were sown, the Court sustained a law providing for sterilization of mentally defective persons.[4] So dubious were the criteria for involuntary sterilization that more than half of the adult male population was vulnerable to the statute's sweep.[5] Despite the enactment's manifest deficiencies and highly invasive reach, the Court dismissed the suggestion of a constitutional violation. Justice Holmes characterized the claim of equal protection, which eventually would become a major source of constitutional doctrine, as a sign of desperation and, in especially memorable terms, gratuitously endorsed of the law by observing that "three generations of imbeciles are enough."[6] Several years later, finding that forced sterilization of repeated criminal offenders was contrary to extraconstitutional values the Court established the foundation upon which the right of privacy would be constructed. Two more decades would elapse before the concept evolved into a clearly articulable principle.[7]

The determination that the First, Third, Fourth, Fifth and Ninth amendments have penumbras forming a repository for the right of privacy,[8] has been denounced for creating a basic right out of thin air[9] and a source of law uncontrolled by any objective limiting principles.[10] Criticism that the right of privacy suddenly materialized as a matter of judicial whim disregards its gradual seepage into the nation's value system. Stripped to its essentials, the decision reflects an accurate response to a widely held belief. The purported discovery of penumbras as constitutional storehouses for value derived principle may have been calculated to avoid appearances of subjectivity, but it delivered more imagery than substance. Efforts to make it appear that the constitution is speaking for itself, or the judiciary is merely deciphering its text or inferring from its structure, are destined to seem contrived or foolish. Eventual placement of the right of privacy within the meaning of liberty secured by the Fourteenth Amendment[11] represents an implicit admission that penumbras or emanations were largely a product of the Court's imagination rather than an inevitability of the constitution itself. Even if insecure with its own function, as evidenced by the need to make its own design appear to be a constitutional original, the result has passed the test for determining a legitimate exercise of power. The right of privacy has endured as constitutional law, not because it is housed in penumbras, but because it flows from values that are widely subscribed to and the principle thus is broadly endorsed.

Because the constitution announces rights in broad terms and contains relatively few specifically prohibitive terms, opportunities abound for manipulation without regard to whether review is styled as activist or restrained. Objections to intervention without an explicit textual command or clear implication disregards a basic reality, noted early by Chief Justice Marshall, that a constitution required to possess all details of rights and powers "could scarcely be embraced by the human mind."[12] A theory of review that precludes reference to external values as a basis for constructing fundamental law, and facilitates forced sterilization or other ignominies, may yield a legacy better forgotten than remembered.

If not to be burdened by the omission of specifics in a charter that was supposed to secure imprecisely formulated concepts of liberty and equality,[13] successive generations must assume significant responsibility not only for vitalizing its "great objects"[14] but identifying what those "great objects" are. Like the founders who composed the constitution, those responsible for its evolution must be attuned and responsive to the citizenry's concerns. Ideally, that sensitivity will be cognizant of rather than blind to the reality of cultural pluralism. Constitutional vitalization is a task that requires not only a grasp of text and structure but the adaptive skills necessary to make it persistently relevant to a diverse society.

Debate over appropriate reference points in crafting basic law tends to note dangers that are more imagined than real. The Court has evinced an increasing reluctance to pursue external value inquiry and a lack of self-certainty when it does. To the extent it has deviated too radically from dominant ideals, jurisprudence invariably is reined in by the unabating pull of popular sentiment. Because text is neither self-defining nor necessarily instructive with respect to its usage, importation of values and introduction of principles referenced to them should be neither avoided nor apologized for on a wholesale basis. Serious incidents of perverse engraftment tend to be easily identified because the instances of distortion, even if profound in impact, are relatively few in number and eventually were corrected or recalibrated to satisfy popular preferences. Drawing upon outside values to activate the constitution need not

be regarded reflexively as an antidemocratic menace, especially insofar as review takes seriously the obligation to explain its results.
In actuality, value-based inquiry has proceeded with such caution
and sensitivity to majoritarian interests that it invites criticism for
catering too much to popular impulse.

The delineation of constitutional principles from external
values is a process that the Court may not always be comfortable
with but which has produced results that lend themselves to
approval at the bottom line. Activism that fashions principle from
external values has been critical to effectuating important rights to
vote, travel and privacy that often are presumed to be enumerated
by the constitution itself. For many, it is surprising to learn that
freedom of association is an implied rather than express right. The
Court considered it "beyond debate that freedom to engage in
association for the advancement of beliefs and ideas" was a constitutionally protected liberty interest.[15] Freedom to associate, it concluded, was inextricably linked to the effectuation of enumerated
freedoms of speech, press and the right to peaceably assemble.[16]

Realistically the right is not inextricable or beyond dispute, insofar as it was manufactured by the Court rather than ordained by
the constitution. Justice Black, who a few years later would object
noisily to the concept of constitutional penumbras or emanations,
himself found freedom of association implicit in the First Amendment.[17] Like other principles grafted to the constitution, it was
born by the press of circumstances rather than the document itself.
Freedom of association vitalized the charter in a way that prevented
Southern officials, seeking to obtain and publicize the names of civil
rights organizers and supporters, from crippling their activity.[18]
Associational freedom undeniably facilitates textually identified
First Amendment interests. It also may be difficult to imagine the
First Amendment functioning as effectively without such an extension. Still, the principle was not in the constitution until the Court
put it there. Although freedom of association was imported rather
than produced from within the document's four corners, it has been
poorly received only by those whose strategy for impeding the civil
rights movement was foiled.

Constitutional embellishment referenced to outside values has proved essential not only in recognizing unenumerated rights but effectuating textually itemized ones. Such a process may entail engraftment of a facilitative rather than entirely independent concept, but the analytical methodology is much the same. Central to the rights of the accused, for instance, are Fourth Amendment guarantees against unreasonable searches and seizures, the Fifth Amendment privilege against self-incrimination and Sixth Amendment right to counsel. Because those provisions also are not self-executing, the Court has formulated constitutional subprinciples to vitalize them. Awareness of the nature and effect of police practices, rather than any directive by the constitution itself, has begotten the exclusionary rule[19] and *Miranda* warnings[20] to help secure the respective efficacy of the Fourth, Fifth and Sixth amendments.

The exclusionary rule under certain circumstances precludes use at trial of illegally seized evidence.[21] The mandate of *Miranda* is that police before commencing custodial interrogation must provide the suspect with warnings of the right to remain silent, the usability at trial of any statements made, and the right to have counsel present and, if necessary, paid for by the state.[22] Neither constitutional subprinciple emerged without considerable forethought or sensitivity to competing concerns. Characteristic of the usual cautious approach toward identifying and delineating constitutional law, they evolved slowly as the Court sought mechanisms that would safeguard basic rights but not interfere unduly with police activity or undermine interests in federalism.

It was the persistent failure of alternative methodologies effectively to secure the underlying guarantees that eventually led toward the constitutional standards which now govern police practices. The resulting criteria not only evolved incrementally and carefully but have been defined and applied since with a sharp eye toward popular sentiment.

The exclusionary rule governed federal criminal procedure for three-quarters of a century before finally being made pertinent to state investigative procedures.[23] Initially, the Court resisted making the Fourth Amendment applicable at all to the states.[24] Even in eventually finding them subject to the prohibition of "unreasonable searches and seizures," the Court balked at incorporating the exclusionary rule.[25] Federalism concerns in part accounted for reticence in expanding the Fourth Amendment's reach, as the Court worried that its demands would cramp state innovation of policies against abusive practices. Noting that most jurisdictions explicitly had rejected the exclusionary rule, the Court concluded that it was not "a departure from basic standards" to leave victims of police misconduct to whatever alternative remedy the states might afford.[26]

It eventually became evident that other options either were unsuccessful in securing Fourth Amendment guarantees or simply were not materializing. Civil remedies proved infeasible because of litigation costs and the credibility disadvantage of a complainant against a police officer. The notion of internal review and discipline by the police generally was a fiction. Only when it became manifest that the states for practical purposes had defaulted upon their obligation to refrain from or deter illegal police practices did the Court finally impose the exclusionary rule upon them.[27]

An extended prelude also antedated the formulation of *Miranda* warnings, which law enforcement officials now must issue to any person subject to custodial interrogation. Although the constitution does not specifically prohibit coerced confessions, the Fifth Amendment affords a privilege against self-incrimination,[28] and the Fourteenth Amendment guarantee due process of law,[29] and the Sixth Amendment creates the right to counsel.[30] *Miranda* and predecessor doctrines reflect concern with interrogation procedures that would subvert those guarantees. Coercive police practices not only deviate from contemporary societal norms and expectations but yield confessions that are inherently suspect.[31]

In originally attempting to embellish and thereby effectuate relevant text, the Court focused upon the circumstances of a confession to determine whether it was voluntary and thereby likely to be reliable.[32] Because actual facts concerning what transpired in the secrecy of interrogation were difficult to ascertain, such an inquiry too often occurred in a vacuum. Consequently, the Court constructed a rule that excluded from evidence confessions received from suspects whose presentation to a judicial officer was unreasonably delayed.[33] Underlying its conclusion was the sense that prompt judicial involvement would deny police the opportunity to isolate and work coercively on a person. The prompt appearance requirement evoked criticism, however, that it impaired even legitimate questioning and freed criminals as a result of police error.[34] The Court thus continued to search for a subprinciple that would actuate the constitution but not unduly interfere with police duties and activities. After briefly experimenting with a requirement of counsel at the police station house,[35] the Court framed the affirmative and prophylactic but minimally burdensome set of warnings that police now must provide.

Like the exclusionary rule, *Miranda* warnings evolved from an initial recognition that the relevant documental guarantees were not self-executing and evolving awareness that constitutional interests were being derogated or underserved by alternative methodologies. Both concepts represent the work of extreme caution and even reticence. The deliberative way in which they emerged and the meticulous justification and outer-directed explanation of them contributed significantly to their ultimate feasibility. Explication that is persuasive and compelling rather than conclusory evinces a judiciary that, even if unelected, is sensitive toward rather than heedless of the citizenry it serves. Such expoundment reflects a process predicated upon accountability.

The exclusionary and *Miranda* rules each were fashioned slowly and pursuant to an accumulation of evidence regarding police abuse that helped secure their viability, despite immediate claims that the Court was soft on criminals and handcuffing the police. The objections are not particularly compelling insofar as it is the constitution which contemplates restrictions upon investigative procedures and the Court merely activated it. Furthermore, few cases are dismissed because of illegally seized evidence.[36] Viewed fairly, a primary appeal of the *Miranda* warnings in particular is their practical simplicity and the judiciary's presumption of their efficacy. Still, the Court has responded to rather than ignored popular criticism in a way that has significantly shaped the eventual working of the subprinciples and the overarching textual guarantees themselves. In creating multiple exceptions to both principles, the Court has referred to the costs they impose upon the criminal justice system and society.[37] Although the eventual turn of the principle may be argued with, the Court cannot be chided for insensitivity to popular preference.

Even if the operation of the exclusionary and *Miranda* rules has been narrowed by subsequent case law, their emergence and endurance with modifications testify to the Court's capacity to identify significant needs, relate them to relevant outside values and formulate a principle that has constitutional standing and is congruent with democratic expectations. Law enforcement officials, who derided the concepts as an abusive and meddlesome exercise of power, since have proclaimed the worth and utility of the formulations.[38] Embellishment and effectuation of textually identifiable constitutional principles now is credited with enhancing professionalism, integrity and the quality of police work.[39] Eventual acknowledgment of legitimacy by the Court's harshest critics is a tribute to quality of process, expoundment and actual result. It also reminds that immediate objections to the consequences of judicial review should be assessed carefully to determine whether they are prompted by concern with function or inconvenience of result.

If measured by "electricity of response,"[40] the determination that segregation was unconstitutional may reflect the Court's most prominent role as an importer of values for manufacturing constitutional law. Prior decisions concerning race were no less referenced to outside values. The desegregation decisions proved to be more activist in appearance, however, because they insisted upon significant change rather than continuity. Both the desegregation mandate and the remedies it eventually begot were preceded and characterized by prolonged reticence in identifying and redressing constitutional wrongs. The relatively short-lived era of assertive insistence upon desegregation was prefaced by constitutional law that was hostile or insensitive to any serious concept of racial equality.

Viewed from its inception, the Fourteenth Amendment has had a twisted history that frequently is difficult to reconcile with its underlying aims. Within a few years of its ratification, the Court observed that its "one pervading purpose" was to secure "the freedom of the slave race, the security and firm establishment of that freedom and the protection of the newly made freeman and citizen from the oppression of those who had formerly exercised unlimited dominion over him."[41] Contrary to the usual problems associated with fathoming legislative intent, the core purpose of the Fourteenth Amendment was well-evidenced by its terms and circumstances. Before the turn of the century, the Court nonetheless embraced the separate but equal doctrine which candidly deferred to racist custom. At the same time, it transformed the Fourteenth Amendment primarily into a platform for economic rights. For more than half a century thereafter, official action was allowed to emphasize separation rather than equality.

Nearly two decades of jurisprudential reflection and doctrinal fine tuning preceded the eventual declaration that "Separate [was] . . . inherently unequal."[42] The actual remedying of officially segregated education, once it was declared illegal, also was characterized by a lengthy prefatory phase during which states and communities were afforded the opportunity to conform policy in their own way to constitutional dictate. Only when the pernicious nature of segregation no longer could be ignored, and it became apparent that corrective action would not be forthcoming, did the Court eventually intervene more forcefully on both counts.

Introduction of the desegregation mandate was not an instance of introducing new values to the constitution but replacing ones that had been imported earlier. Several decades elapsed after the embrace of the separate but equal doctrine before the Court acknowledged the accuracy of Justice Harlan's prophesy of its eventual legacy. Harlan had dissented from the concept of separate but equal on grounds it facilitated racial privilege rather than equality and would "in time prove to be . . . as pernicious as" earlier decisions upholding slavery.[43] The Court's original observation, that inferiority was mistakenly inferred by segregation's victims,[44] denoted either a disregard of or total insensitivity toward reality. Official characterization of the separate but equal doctrine as not affecting civil or political equality represented an exercise in raw denial and distortion, even if well-attuned to the impulses of the time.

Regardless of how it was depicted, the separate but equal doctrine countenanced egregious disparities in the apportionment of rights and assignment of status. South Carolina in 1915, for instance, allocated almost ten times more money for white than for black students.[45] By 1954, when separate finally was declared unequal, Southern states still were spending nearly half as much more on white students than on black students.[46] Never, except in the few instances in which the Court insisted upon qualified equalization, did the separate but equal doctrine even pretend to serve equal protection purposes. Rather, it functioned primarily to consolidate and perpetuate those vestiges of a privileged and advantaged system disrupted by the elimination of slavery and ratification of the Fourteenth Amendment.

Repugnant as it may have been, the separate but equal doctrine died a slow death. Eventual dismantling of official segregation was preceded by a few narrowly framed orders directed toward gross inequalities that could not be ignored. It was difficult not to acknowledge after a time, for instance, that the failure to provide an educational opportunity for blacks while one was being afforded whites was constitutionally unequal. The Court thus determined, although not unanimously, that equal protection was denied when a state provided a law school for whites but not for blacks.[47] Even then, accentuation of equality was mild and substantial time would pass before the Court finally concluded that official segregation was constitutionally inconsonant. Meanwhile, the Court ordered another state to create a law school for blacks or offer a legal education for them at its exclusively white university.[48] When the state merely roped off a section of the capitol building and termed it a black law school, the Court denied further relief.[49] The patent inequality of such an arrangement would seem difficult to overlook despite the standards of the time. Although the separate but equal doctrine theoretically might have been reconstituted into a stronger equal protection tonic, at least with respect to equalizing physical facilities and capital outlay, it functioned largely as a constitutional placebo.

Even as the notion that separate never could be equal became increasingly irrefutable, the Court expressed its preference for making constitutional law that would "be drawn as narrowly as possible."[50] Its initial foray into desegregation evinced more reticence than assertiveness, as demonstrated by the narrow and lightly populated area of education upon which it focused. Although soon to recognize that segregation at the elementary school level was especially pernicious,[51] the Court until then departed from the separate but equal doctrine only in the context of graduate and professional education.[52]

In observing that separate seating arrangements impaired the learning process, and a black law school was inferior because it lacked not only capital resources but intangibles such as reputation, prestige and influence, the Court identified disparities actually characterizing all educational levels.[53] Initially nonetheless it declared racial separation only at the highest academic strata to be at odds with concepts of substantial equality.[54]

The evidence of stigmatization and interference with educational opportunity, which the Court eventually found to be particularly significant at the elementary level and grounds for declaring separate inherently unequal,[55] already was within its field of comprehension. Still, it remained tentative and circumspect, as evidenced by the observation that "much of the excellent research and detailed argument in these cases is unnecessary to their disposition."[56] The Court's first articulated reservations about the separate but equal doctrine itself, therefore, were couched in exceedingly narrow terms and applied to an area of education in which the potential for significant racial mixing at the time was minimal.

The eventual order for desegregation at all levels of public education, in 1954, constituted a radical revision of equal protection doctrine. It is unlikely that any judicial decision has insisted upon a more significant societal revision than the mandate for desegregation. Even so, the pronouncement was characterized by a strong sense of self-restraint and deference toward dominant sensitivities. The decision in *Brown v. Board of Education*[57] overtly drew upon outside values to make equal protection terms relevant to a pluralistic society. The Court delved into psychological and sociological studies demonstrating that segregation connoted inferiority and that, contrary to the conclusion of the *Plessy* Court, negative connotations were implied by policy rather than mistakenly inferred by the victim.[58] Social science also led to the constitutionally significant conclusion that separation of children "solely because of their race generates a feeling of inferiority as to their status in the community that may affect their hearts and minds in a way unlikely ever to be undone."[59]

As a consequence, the Court found separate educational facilities so clearly violative of equal protection that examination of an accompanying due process challenge was unnecessary. The constitutional predicate for desegregation, which several decades earlier would have been dismissed as a sign of litigative desperation, thus had evolved into a principle of first choice.

Because evidence of the harmful consequences of racial separation had been available to the Court for many years, the desegregation mandate was anything but rushed or impulsive. Conscious of both the incendiary potential of the principle and its own inability to force compliance, the Court was alert to the sensitivities of those who would have to alter their established customs and ways. Rather than demanding immediate compliance, it put off for a full term even providing a remedy. The delay was calculated to afford federal and state governments an opportunity to supply ideas on how to contour relief.[60] The consequent order for desegregation "with all deliberate speed"[61] on its face acknowledged the diverse and unique circumstances in which the mandate would operate. More profoundly if not explicitly stated, it also represented a sense that the viability of the principle depended upon its capacity to command widespread popular support. Thus, the Court immediately began soliciting state and local cooperation and participation in adapting the new constitutional principle to community realities. Remediation thus was characterized by as much care and reserve as the underlying principle's formulation.

What followed, despite efforts to secure cooperation rather than confrontation, was widespread resistance, delay and evasion by state and local officials aided and abetted by mutinous lower courts.[62] Some school districts, recognizing that litigation was necessary to alter the status quo and that potential plaintiffs generally had inadequate resources to contest segregation, merely ignored the decree. Laws providing for disbarment of civil rights attorneys were designed to minimize further the possibility of challenges to established ways.[63] Common reactions also included sham desegregation plans. Freedom of choice and provisions for student transfer policies helped fortify customary social patterns against elimination of laws that previously had supported them.[64]

The desegregation order also reignited old sectional antagonisms akin to those that divided and embattled the union a century earlier. Arkansas, for instance, attempted to resurrect the principle of state rights by enacting a law intended to free students from compulsory attendance at biracial schools.[65] It accordingly amended its constitution so that the legislature was required to give final approval to the "Unconstitutional desegregation decision."[66] Desegregation in those circumstances, like the eradication of slavery before, was accomplished ultimately by federal force of arms.

In initially ordering desegregation, the Court had calibrated the operation of constitutional law to its sense of what the realities of forced change demanded. Resistance, subterfuge and delay nevertheless constituted the norm for official responses to the mandate. A decade later, only 2 percent of black students in the states originally affected by desegregation attended schools where they were not a racial majority.[67] The Court's efforts were further sabotaged by lower federal courts, which formulated concepts designed to obstruct desegregation and secure established racist institutions and practices.[68] Their cheerleading for ways which had been declared unconstitutional facilitated official avoidance of legal responsibility. Although the entry point for challenges to unconstitutional practices, the lower courts became self-appointed guardians of a competing value system based upon entrenched racism. Delay, tokenism and disregard continued for fifteen years until the Court finally concluded that "The time for mere 'deliberate' speed has run out."[69] Just as the original desegregation order had followed an extended prologue, the Court's eventual insistence upon a plan that "promises realistically to work *now*"[70] was preceded by a long waiting period that ended only upon recognition that further intervention was required if equal protection aims were to be fulfilled.

Judicial commencement of the desegregation process notwithstanding, it was the elected branches of federal government which voluntarily embraced and enforced the Court's constitutional mandate and affixed to it an incontrovertible imprint of democratic consent. The Civil Rights Act of 1964 authorized the Justice Department to file desegregation suits[71] and thereby diminished the possibility that segregation would persist for lack of means to challenge it. Pursuant to the 1964 Act, which barred federal assistance for any program administered in a racially discriminatory fashion, the Department of Health, Education and Welfare conditioned aid to school districts upon their compliance with duties to desegregate.[72] A panoply of other congressional enactments secured civil rights and equal opportunity in employment, voting, housing, public accommodations, education and other areas which like education had been formally segregated or exclusionary.[73]

Although the Court may have taken the lead in declaring segregation unlawful, the more directly representative branches of government formulated the critical effectuating policies and supplied force when necessary to secure relevant principles. When President Eisenhower dispatched federal troops to Little Rock to enforce the desegregation decree, it was not just the judiciary but the executive branch signaling that the Court's constitutional pronouncements were the supreme law of the land.[74] Such a claim would have had purely rhetorical value if the states' contentions rather than the Court's expoundments had captured the sympathy of the President or Congress. Effective supremacy in the area of desegregation thus proved contingent upon cooperation of and endorsement by the coordinate branches of government and direct agents of the citizenry.

Implementation of the desegregation mandate was neither long-lived nor unresponsive to popular sentiment. As the focus upon segregated schools expanded northward and westward, and remedial busing of students became an increasingly divisive issue, the eventual reach of the desegregation principle became an increasingly prominent political concern. It was a critical element of the 1968 presidential campaign, as George Wallace packaged his strident opposition to desegregation into a candidacy that siphoned off enough Democratic votes to make Richard Nixon triumphant. Nixon himself had objected publicly to busing and appended his criticism with the promise to appoint strict constructionists to the Court.[75] Implicit was a pledge to appoint judges with less fertile equal protection imaginations, who would be less inclined to order busing or other aggressive remedies disquieting to majoritarian concerns.

Coinciding with increasingly palpable public concern with the eventual reach of desegregation and forcefulness of means to effectuate it, and Nixon's transformation of the Warren Court into the Burger Court, a set of limiting principles emerged that largely would gut much of the mandate's potential. Since 1954, American society had become increasingly mobile as freeways and suburban development reshaped population centers. Especially in metropolitan areas, segregation at least on the surface could be seen as a function of residence rather than official action. Movement into new communities tracked along wealth lines which generally paralleled racial lines. The result was a perpetuation of racial separation attributable to forces not clearly contemplated by the *Brown* Court, which had focused upon officially prescribed sequestration. Instead of concentrating upon the underlying causes of residential segregation, the Court referred to superficial circumstances as a basis for reconstituting the desegregation principle into a less potent formula. As a consequence, pervasive racial separation in American schools was placed largely beyond the ken of constitutional concern and desegregation became a largely optional rather than constitutional pursuit.

The first key principle limiting the duty to desegregate conditioned it upon proof that racial separation was the product of official intent.[76] To the extent racial separation could be attributed to factors other than what the Court determined to be purposeful, desegregation would not be required. The distinction between de jure and de facto segregation, even if more illusory than real, was a crucial one. By essentially excluding residential segregation from constitutional purview, the Court relieved much of the North and West from any desegregation obligations.

The exemption significantly undercut the potential reach of desegregation but the etching of constitutional lines seems to have been guided by logic that was primarily political. Residential segregation when closely examined is as much a descendant of intentional discrimination as the formal segregation policies which the Court had condemned. Patterns of migration and settlement were influenced by government action which, until 1948, enforced restrictive covenants[77] and, thereafter, continued to foster racially discrete neighborhoods pursuant to official red-lining policies.[78] The Federal Housing Administration, which was a major source of mortgage financing and primary force behind suburban development and settlement, considered racial mixing an adverse influence upon neighborhoods. Given FHA rules prohibiting loans that would contribute to racially diverse neighborhoods,[79] official action was instrumental in establishing and maintaining residential segregation.

Further contributing toward those ends were official decisions concerning the location of public housing and schools and distribution of urban development funds.[80] Officially abetted or condoned violence, in some instances, also helped maintain racially separate neighborhoods.[81] Although perhaps not as blatantly discriminatory as laws requiring racial separation, the purpose and effect of such policies and actions were indistinguishable.

Despite the linkage between intentional state action and residential segregation, the Court found the consequences to be constitutionally tolerable. It thereby erected against future legal challenges to segregated schools the nearly insurmountable obstacle of proving discriminatory intent. Illegal motive when not overt is highly elusive. Facially routine decisions regarding school sitings and closings, attendance zones, neighborhood policies, faculty hiring, assignment and promotion, transfer policies, curriculum, educational tracks and social, athletic and recreational policies all have ample hiding room for racism that is subtle rather than overt. Wrongful intent as a standard of review in any constitutional setting has been rightly condemned. Even those who apply it in the equal protection area have been quick to criticize it elsewhere.[82] Efforts to determine illegal purpose behind policies governing religion, expression and commerce regularly have been depicted as vain because a collective intent seldom exists.[83] If a motive is unlawful, moreover, it likely will be disguised. Selective application of the discriminatory intent standard, to curtail desegregation's potential, thus invited characterization as a principle of convenience and concession to majoritarian concern.[84]

If viewed as a rule of utility, discriminatory intent is not unlike the concept of proximate cause which limits a person's liability for negligence primarily out of concern for the consequences of not doing so. Both notions cut off responsibility at some point to ensure liability does not extend indefinitely. Although equal educational opportunity was a primary concern of the original desegregation mandate,[85] the Court later acknowledged intervening political realities and factored them into constitutional doctrine.

As the focus upon segregation expanded to include the entire nation, logic might have dictated that separate schools were evil regardless of causal externalities.[86] Instead, discriminatory intent became the basis for a double standard requiring mostly regional change. Its emergence and operation, instead of a comprehensive accounting for all segregation, was more evocative of a legalism than of a clear view of history and appreciation of cause. It nonetheless enabled the judiciary to avoid or defuse majoritarian distress that a less differentiating mandate probably would have enhanced. What were presented as constitutional lines of distinction more accurately were boundaries of convenience reflecting the Court's sense of reaching the outer limits of its authority in a society disposed toward functional if not official segregation.

Further responsive to majoritarian sentiment was the Court's determination that interdistrict remedies were not allowable unless state or suburban officials actively and proximately had facilitated segregation.[87] The significant post–*Brown* forces of personal mobility and suburban development, as previously noted, shaped a societal landscape different from what the Court originally examined in ordering desegregation. Families that left the cities and formed predominantly if not exclusively white suburban rings did so not by force of law but because they could afford it.[88] The shrinking tax base and deteriorating conditions occasioned by their departure created an accelerating population redistribution that increasingly made urban desegregation orders practical fictions.

Objectives identified by the *Brown* Court actually had little time to be pursued much less accomplished within the community structure it had considered. Although the societal framework over the next couple of decades was fluid and dynamic, constitutional doctrine proved elastic only in the capacity to shrink in relationship to its context. While educational equalization interests increasingly were being subverted by the drift toward better funded, mostly white suburban schools and underfunded, largely black urban schools,[89] constitutional law retreated further into narrowly conceived standards of actionability. Educational equality even at the most rudimentary level proved to be a constitutional irrelevancy, as funding disparities in some instances became reminiscent of those in the South toward the end of the separate but equal doctrine's reign.[90]

For desegregation to have reached its full potential, equal protection doctrine would have had to be recalibrated for altered circumstances. Given such an opportunity, the Court nonetheless declined it in a politically conscious and calculating decision. Notwithstanding the nature and underlying cause of metropolitan settlement patterns, the Court concluded that interdistrict remedies were not required absent a showing of one district's intent to discriminate against another.[91] In reversing the lower court's order for busing between city and suburban schools, the Court dismissed evidentiary findings of transcendent discrimination although it acknowledged the operation of discriminatory purpose within the school district itself.[92] Consequently, the Court's second significant limiting principle ensured that desegregation remedies would not likely affect those mainly white families who had left the city for the suburbs.

The shift in emphasis and tone was not without irony. Lower courts, which for two decades had been rebuked for not moving fast or far enough in effectuating desegregation, were suddenly admonished for their excessive haste and reach.[93] Censure for subverting the original desegregation mandate thus was transformed into reproach for missing the beat of the Court's revised agenda.

By largely sanctifying school district lines and effectively insulating suburban education from desegregation, the Court retreated further from the fullest implications of *Brown*. Desegregation as a consequence became an even more remote prospect for modern society. For constitutional interests to be implicated, it first was necessary to clear the imposing barrier of proving discriminatory intent. If that hurdle was cleared, remediation was not especially meaningful if a school district was populated primarily by citizens of a single race. Even assuming those obstacles to meaningful relief were surmounted, introduction of a third limiting principle established an impediment to lasting relief. The Court's final constricting twist of the desegregation mandate made the constitutional duties flowing from it essentially transient. Once a school system subject to a desegregation order was declared unitary, officials would not be obligated to adjust policy to resegregation unless a new discriminatory intent was proved.[94]

The decision signified that even if segregation existed and constitutional attention initially was required the Court would not be concerned if the condition recurred as a consequence of population redistribution. Most modern variants of racial separation thus had been safely removed from the constitution's potential reach.

The denouement of the desegregation mandate represented a

logical windup for doctrinal travel that had commenced with the conditioning of desegregative duties upon proof of official intent. Once the linkage to state action was cut, at least to the Court's satisfaction, resegregation would be attributed to what was described as the "quite normal pattern of human migration."[95] The principle thus devolved to a point where the Court's language was hauntingly reminiscent of terminology it had employed in characterizing segregation as being "in the nature of things."[96] Given the heavy concentration of blacks in cities and whites in suburbs, the narrowing of grounds and remedies for desegregation effectively guarantees "that Negro children . . . will receive the same separate and inherently unequal education in the future as they have been unconstitutionally afforded in the past."[97] That reality proved subordinate to the force of majoritarian gravity, however, as an influence upon the direction of constitutional law.

The desegregation era, viewed as a whole, was slow in coming and relatively quick to exit. During a relatively brief period of forceful application, however, it contributed to a significant restructuring of the South and ultimately facilitated political change there. Despite the calculated neglect of the desegregation mandate's potential and popular distress that *Brown* and its progeny engendered, a dominant sense undoubtedly would be that invalidation of segregation was as right as endorsement of slavery was wrong. The contrition and confessions of some notably hard-line segregationists further testify to the pertinence and validity of the values upon which desegregation was predicted. George Wallace's active pursuit of black voters, within two decades after personally manning segregation barricades at the University of Alabama, testify to the altered political realities that the desegregation mandate helped facilitate.

Altered conventions and eventual investment in or accommodation to the values imported for constitutional processing suggest eventual consent even from what initially were the Court's most strident critics. Insofar as desegregation would have been without significant popular support and compelling explanations for expanding its political base, the Court would have been subject to intense pressure not just to narrow but retract it. As decisions concerning economic rights earlier this century and abortion now demonstrate, judicial restructuring proposals and persistent challenges are the litany of judgments reflecting seriously and persistently controverted values. Many threats have been made against the judiciary but few actually have been acted upon. Even if its underlying motives are not absolutely provable, the Court consistently has demonstrated a knack for charting or recalibrating doctrine in a way that defuses the potential for political conflict. It should not be surprising, therefore, that the history of desegregation is replaying itself with respect to affirmative action principles. Increasingly restrictive allowances for racial preferences in hiring, education and other avenues evince again the contouring of doctrine consonant with majoritarian predilections.[98]

Objection to the gutting of a doctrine that was overdue in its arrival and stunted in its growth is understandable. The sensitivity to popular sentiment that accounted for the trilogy of limiting principles that emerged, however, defuses notions of the judiciary as an antidemocratic institution. Decisions that curbed the potential reach of desegregation may rest upon dubious calculations and appraisals, but they show a Court that is strongly preoccupied with majoritarian preferences. Such sensitivity is not unique in the contouring of constitutional law. The evolution of other documental adornments, including the exclusionary rule, *Miranda* requirements and right of privacy, shows an inclination to author decisions with a finger on society's pulse rather than just an eye to logical implication or actual cause and effect. Doctrinal elasticity notable for its shrinkage rather than expansion denotes a sense of accountability that is sensitive toward rather than heedless of the need for popular consent. Contrary to the imagery projected by the judiciary's detractors, reality evidences an institution tightly bound to dominant sentiments. Constitutional law is more vulnerable to criticism that is overly responsive to majoritarian or orthodox impulses and neglectful of cultural pluralism.[99]

A tendency to float in mainstream sentiment is not the trait of an institution perilous to democracy. What is evident instead is a function that is sufficiently controlled, if not excessively so, and at least more appealing in its present form than under influences that would curtail further or distort function and principle. Even if cut from the Court's rather than constitution's cloth, externally referenced principles of constitutional law reveal a distinctly majoritarian weave posing little practical threat to democratic values.

# References

1. *See* Brownstein, *With or Without Supreme Court Changes, Reagan Will Reshape the Federal Bench*, 49 NAT'L. J. 2338, 2340 (1984).
2. Warren and Brandeis, *The Right to Privacy*, 4 HARV. L. REV. 193 (1890).
3. *See Skinner v. Oklahoma*, 316 U.S. 535 (1942).
4. *See Buck v. Bell*, 274 U.S. 200 (1927).
5. *See* L. TRIBE, GOD SAVE THIS HONORABLE COURT 13 (1985).
6. *See Buck v. Bell*, 274 U.S. at 207–08.
7. *See Griswold v. Connecticut*, 381 U.S. 479 (1965).
8. *Griswold v. Connecticut*, 381 U.S. at 481–86.
9. Brownstein, *supra* note 1.
10. *See, e.g.*, J. NOWAK, R. ROTUNDA & J. YOUNG, CONSTITUTIONAL LAW, §11.7, at 368 (1986).
11. *See, e.g., Moore v. City of East Cleveland*, 431 U.S. 494–499 (1977); *Roe v. Wade*, 410 U.S. 113, 152 (1973).
12. *McCulloch v. Maryland*, 17 U.S. (4 Wheat.) 316, 407 (1819).
13. *See* U.S. CONST., Preamble.
14. *McCulloch v. Maryland*, 17 U.S. (4 Wheat) 316, 418 (1819).
15. *NAACP v. Alabama*, 357 U.S. 449, 460 (1958).
16. *See id.*
17. *See id.*
18. *See id.*
19. *See Mapp v. Ohio*, 367 U.S. 643, 651–63 (1961).
20. *See Miranda v. Arizona*, 384 U.S. 436, 445–58 (1966).
21. *Mapp v. Ohio*, 367 U.S. at 655.
22. *Miranda v. Arizona*, 384 U.S. at 467–73.
23. *Boyd v. United States*, 116 U.S. 616 (1886).
24. *Weeks v. United States*, 232 U.S. 383, 394 (1914).
25. *Wolf v. Colorado*, 338 U.S. 25, 33 (1949).
26. *Id.* at 32–33.
27. *See Mapp v. Ohio*, 367 U.S. 643.
28. U.S. CONST., amend. V.
29. U.S. CONST., amend. V and XIV.
30. U.S. CONST., amend. VI.

31. See *Rogers v. Richmond*, 365 U.S. 534 (1961).
32. See *Brown v. Mississippi*, 297 U.S. 278 (1936).
33. See *Mallory v. United States*, 354 U.S. 449 (1957).
34. See W. LAFAVE & J. ISRAEL, CRIMINAL PROCEDURE 271 (1985).
35. See *Escobedo v. Illinois*, 378 U.S. 478 (1964).
36. See *United States v. Leon*, 468 U.S. 897, 940-42 (Brennan, J., dissenting).
37. See, e.g., *id.*; *New York v. Quarles*, 467 U.S. 649, 656-57 (1984).
38. Raven, *Crime and the Bill of Rights: Separating Myth from Reality*, 74 A.B.A.J. 8, 8 (Nov. 1, 1988).
39. *Id.*
40. A.T. MASON, THE SUPREME COURT FROM TAFT TO WARREN 180 (1958).
41. Slaughter-House Cases, 83 U.S. (16 Wall.) 36, 71 (1873).
42. *Brown v. Board of Education*, 347 U.S. at 493.
43. *Plessy v. Ferguson*, 163 U.S. 537, 559 (1896) (Harlan, J., dissenting).
44. *Id.* at 551.
45. See A. LEWIS, PORTRAIT OF A DECADE: THE SECOND AMERICAN REVOLUTION 20 (1964).
46. See *id.*
47. Missouri ex rel. *Gaines v. Canada*, 305 U.S. 337, 345 (1938).
48. *Sipuel v. Board of Regents*, 332 U.S. 631, 633 (1948).
49. *Fisher v. Hurst*, 333 U.S. 147 (1948).
50. *Sweatt v. Painter*, 339 U.S. 629, 631 (1950).
51. See *Brown v. Board of Education*, 347 U.S. 383 494-95 (1954).
52. See *McLaurin v. Oklahoma State Regents for Higher Education*, 339 U.S. 637 (1950); *Sweatt v. Painter*, 339 U.S. 629.
53. McLaurin, 339 U.S. at 641; Sweatt, 339 U.S. at 633-34.
54. McLaurin, 339 U.S. at 641-42; Sweatt, 339 U.S. at 633-34.
55. See *Brown v. Board of Education*, 347 U.S. at 494-95.
56. *Sweatt v. Painter*, 339 U.S. at 631.
57. 347 U.S. 483.
58. *Plessy v. Ferguson*, 163 U.S. at 551.
59. *Brown v. Board of Education*, 347 U.S. at 494.
60. *Brown v. Board of Education*, 349 U.S. 294, 301 (1955).
61. *Id.*
62. See II N. DORSEN, P. BENDER, B. NEUBORNE & S. LAW, POLITICAL AND CIVIL RIGHTS IN THE UNITED STATES, CH. XXVIII, 625-43 (1976); A. LEWIS, *supra* note 45, at 29-59, 102-06, 134-51, 251-58.
63. See *NAACP v. Button*, 371 U.S. 415 (1963).
64. See *Green v. County School Board*, 391 U.S. 430, 439-42 (1968); *Goss v. Board of Education*, 373 U.S. 683, 685-87 (1963).
65. See *Cooper v. Aaron*, 358 U.S. 11, 8-9 (1958).
66. *Id.*
67. BUREAU OF THE CENSUS: U.S. DEPT. OF COMMERCE, STATISTICAL ABSTRACT OF THE UNITED STATES 124 (1974).
68. Federal district courts actually facilitated southern resistance by endorsing

plans designed not to work and creating procedural hurdles, such as those requiring a plaintiff to exhaust administrative remedies, before bringing an action in federal court. *See United States v. Jefferson County Board of Education,* 372 F. 2d 836, 863 (5th Cir. 1966); *McNeese v. Board of Education,* 373 U.S. 668 (1963).

69. *Green v. County School Board,* 391 U.S. at 439.

70. *Id.* (emphasis in original).

71. W. DORSEN, P. BENDER, B. NEUBORNE & S. LAW, *supra* note 62, Ch. XXVIII, 633–43 (1976).

72. *See id.*

73. *See* Civil Rights Acts of 1968, 1964 and 1957; Voting Rights Act of 1957.

74. *Cooper v. Aaron,* 358 U.S. at 18.

75. *See* B. SCHWARTZ, SWANN'S WAY: THE SCHOOL BUSING CASE AND THE SUPREME COURT 186–89 (1986).

76. *See Keyes v. School District No. 1,* 413 U.S. 189, 205–14 (1973).

77. *See Shelley v. Kraemer,* 334 U.S. 19 (1948).

78. *See* P. JACOBS, PRELUDE TO RIOT: A VIEW OF URBAN AMERICA FROM THE BOTTOM 139–41 (1967).

79. *See id.*; G. MYRDAL, AN AMERICAN DILEMMA 625 (1962).

80. *See Keyes v. School District No. 1,* 413 U.S. at 216; Karst, *Not One Rule at Rome and Another at Athens: The Fourteenth Amendment in Nationwide Application,* 1972 WASH. U.L.Q. 383, 388–89.

81. *See, e.g.,* W. TUTTLE, JR., RACE RIOT: CHICAGO IN THE RED SUMMER OF 1919 157–83 (1970); S. DRAKE & H. CAYTON, BLACK METROPOLIS 174–82 (1945).

82. *See, e.g., Kassel v. Consolidated Freightways, Corp.,* 450 U.S. 662, 702–03 (1981) (Rehnquist, J., dissenting).

83. *United States v. O'Brien,* 391 U.S. 367, 383–84 (1968).

84. *See Keyes v. School District No. 1,* 413 U.S. at 218–19 and nn. 3–4 (Powell, J., concurring and dissenting).

85. *See Brown v. Board of Education,* 347 U.S. at 493. *See also* Bell, *Serving Two Masters: Integration Ideals and Client Interests in School Desegregation Litigation,* 85 YALE L.J. 470, 487–88 (1976).

86. *See Keyes v. School District No. 1,* 413 U.S. at 718–19 and nn. 3–4 (Powell, J., concurring and dissenting).

87. *Milliken v. Bradley,* 418 U.S. 717, 746–47 (1974).

88. *See* L. TRIBE, AMERICAN CONSTITUTIONAL LAW 1042 (1978).

89. The public school systems in Washington, D.C. and Baltimore, for instance, had become more than 90 percent black. *See Riddick v. School Board of City of Norfolk,* 784 F. 2d 521, 528 (4th Cir.), *cert. denied,* 107 S.Ct. 420 (1986). Detroit's public school population was more than 70 percent black and growing. *See Milliken v. Bradley,* 433 U.S. 267, 271 n.3 (1977). Average pupil expenditures in Ohio's three largest cities were approximately $3,000, compared to over $4,000 in nearby white suburbs. STATE OF OHIO, DEPARTMENT OF EDUCATION, COSTS PER PUPIL, Table 1, at 5, 7–8 and Table 2, at 28, 30–31 (1984–85).

90. *See supra* note 45–46, and accompanying text–46.

91. *Milliken v. Bradley,* 418 U.S. at 745; 767–72 (White, J., dissenting).

92. *Id.* at 746–47.

93. *Compare Swann v. Charlotte-Mecklenburg Board of Education*, 402 U.S. 1, 25 (1971); *Davis v. School Commissioner*, 402 U.S. 33, 37 (1971); *Green v. County School Board*, 391 U.S. 430, 439 (1968) with *Milliken v. Bradley*, 418 U.S. at 745.
94. *Pasadena City Board of Education v. Spangler*, 427 U.S. 424, 437 (1976).
95. *Id.* at 436.
96. *Plessy v. Ferguson*, 163 U.S. at 551.
97. *Milliken v. Bradley*, 418 U.S. at 782 (Marshall, J., dissenting).
98. *See, e.g., City of Richmond v. J.A. Croson Company*, 109 S.Ct. 706 (1989).
99. *See FCC v. Pacifica Foundation*, 437 U.S. 726, (Brennan, J., dissenting).

# Five

# Judicial Subjectivism: Occupational Hazards of a Constitutional Society

The judiciary almost invariably is maligned when it enunciates law from borrowed value rather than from the constitution itself. It is easy but seldom compelling, when aggrieved by the outcome of such review, to allege that power and process have been abused. Critical demeanor has a way of evaporating in the light of a more convenient outcome or when a point or agenda of profound personal interest is at stake. The Court, for instance, has recognized "that the constitution protects the sanctity of the family" because it is "deeply rooted in . . . history and tradition" and is an institution through which "many of our most cherished values" are passed down. [1] Predictably, the conclusion has been criticized as judge-made law having no ties to the constitution's text or design.[2] Equally unsurprising, many who chided the Court for referencing constitutional principle to family values have advanced them as grounds for eliminating or narrowing abortion rights.[3]

Hypocrisy thus is a common denominator of both urgings and criticisms of judicial intervention. Regardless of how the constitution is embellished, abiding disaffection with judicially chosen values and predicates invariably induces reexamination and revision of principle. Such was the history of contractual liberty, the separate but equal doctrine and the desegregation mandate. It now may be the future of abortion rights. Actual doctrinal change may not be immediate and may require politically inspired appointments to the judiciary. Persistent challenge to the Court's engraftments, in any event, is one of democracy's ways of signaling its interest in further evaluation and perhaps recalibration of the law.[4]

The Court itself has allowed that it "is most vulnerable and comes nearest to illegitimacy when it deals with judge-made law having little or no cognizable roots in the language or design of the constitution."[5] Such an observation accompanied the Court's refusal to expand privacy rights and thereby bar a state from criminalizing homosexual activity between consenting adults.[6] The intimation that a contrary result would be unrooted in or marginally tied to the constitution's text or structure consciously or unconsciously invested in the myth that the document somehow communicates with and guides the Court. In reality the Court's conclusion reflected a choice between competing sets of values independent of the constitution. Priorities not set by the document itself and generally reflecting a sense of dominant preference thus determined the reach of privacy rights.

Further evidencing the decision's inspiration by imported value rather than scriptural instruction is the simplicity with which a contrary but defensible result could be reached. Ample precedent exists for constitutionally acknowledging a personal freedom to make choices concerning intimate aspects of life.[7] If the Court had depicted the issue as a matter of bedroom privacy or personal autonomy, the question of homosexuality would have been subsumed by the broader characterization and constitutional protection would have been a logical extension. Description of the claim in terms of asserting a "fundamental right to engage in homosexual sodomy,"[8] however, intimates a result-oriented coloration.

Because modern constitutional engrafting purports to be governed by whether the relevant concern or interest is implicit in a concept of ordered liberty or deeply rooted in the nation's conscience, characterization of the issue in terms of a right of privacy or right to pursue homosexual activity is critical to the point of being outcome determinative. While privacy may be implicit in liberty or etched in conscience, homosexuality by itself is less likely to be. The choice of how to style the issue reveals the values, rather than any constitutional explication or implication, that impelled the Court toward its conclusion and probably minimized its vulnerability to unfavorable popular review. Even if privacy interests suffered, the judgment is another example of decision-making cast in the lexicon of restraint but actually referenced to and facilitative of values.

Judicial restraint in formulating supreme law may be welcome if it merely precludes arbitrary conversion of a political agenda into constitutional edict. It remains deceiving for the Court to submit, however, that it cannot act unless guided by principles textually identified or clearly rooted in the constitution.[9] Such abnegation equates the constitution with scripture which can be activated only by proper scrutiny and deciphering rather than infusion of outside values. In fact, the constitution has no secrets or mysteries waiting to be unlocked. Standards to the effect of whether an interest is implicit in a concept of ordered liberty or rooted in society's conscience may pretend to facilitate the document's revelations, but in reality they are valuable as a means toward judicial accountability for values chosen and principles engrafted. Neither analytical standards nor precedent was incompatible with a judgment that would have contoured the right of privacy to protect homosexual activity. Rejection of that configuration was a consequence not of documental instruction, but more likely of a powerful fear of straying too far from mainstream conventions or risking popular disapproval.[10]

Because key charter terminology is meaningless unless the Court inspires it with external values, it is misleading to declare that a certain result cannot be reached because the constitution does not authorize or allow it.[11] A more honest statement would be that the judiciary has power to chart the substantive perimeters of liberty, equal protection, privileges and immunities and other open-ended constitutional provisions fettered only by the need to secure the approval or tolerance of the citizenry and the rest of the government. Without a successful pitch for the values it has selected and the interests it has elevated to constitutional status, it is difficult to imagine any graft of principle actually remaining fastened over the long run.[12]

Much apprehension regarding the importation of values is attributable to the judiciary's fumbling of the process earlier this century. In *Lochner v. New York*,[13] the Court elevated liberty of contract to the status of a fundamental right and for three decades persistently invoked it to thwart economic and social welfare legislation. The episode is widely regarded as a painful example of rampant subjectivism and judicial abuse. Its legacy is so profoundly negative that contemporary efforts to breathe life into the Fourteenth Amendment almost invariably is impaired by fears and allegations of neo–Lochnerism.[14]

The Court's doctrinal excursions from 1905 to 1937 are commonly criticized as an exercise in judicial caprice. The argument that judicial legitimacy depends upon formulation of principles clearly tied to constitutional text or design, however, is not necessarily inconsonant with Lochnerism and does not account satisfactorily for its deficiencies. Contractual liberty has an arguable connection to the constitution, insofar as the contracts clause provides a textual safeguard against state interference with contractual obligations.[15] Until the late Nineteenth Century, when the Court began to develop the liberty component of the due process clause, the contracts clause was a primary restraint upon state economic regulation.[16] Freedom of contract at least would appear to emanate more readily from the contracts clause than the right of privacy flows from several guarantees in the Bill of Rights.[17] Relative linkage of a principle to actual text or design, as liberty of contract and the right of privacy demonstrate in their own ways, does not necessarily determine the legitimacy of review or the long term viability of the resulting constitutional doctrine.

The Fourteenth Amendment prohibits state government from denying any person "life, liberty, or property, without due process of law."[18] The guarantee neither defines the scope of liberty nor declares the branches of government against which it operates. Because liberty can be compromised by legislative or judicial action, scrutiny of the substantive fairness of laws rather than just the procedural fairness of adjudication has become an established practice. Still, the focus and breadth of such review were not set by the terms of the Fourteenth Amendment and are a continuing source of controversy. Many of the provision's architects regarded liberty of contract as a guarantee essential toward effectuating full terms of citizenship and equality of former slaves.[19] A general concept of economic rights, however, was not fixed at the outset and eventual enunciation of contractual freedom represented an extension of ideology.

The values imported by the Court to embellish liberty at the turn of the century reflected political thought that was common but increasingly disputed. Presidents Harrison, Cleveland and Taft were strong proponents of laissez-faire principles and the interests of private enterprise.[20] Commitment to sheltering those ideals and concerns became a paramount criterion in their screening and selection of judicial nominees.[21] As a consequence, the Court which confronted the Twentieth Century was programmed to champion marketplace freedom and view dimly the burgeoning social and economic reforms propagated by the increasingly popular but competing philosophy of progressivism.

Liberty of contract did not become a fundamental right pursuant to a meticulous or dispassionate inquiry into whether it was implicit in a concept of ordered liberty or rooted in the nation's traditions and conscience. Rather, the notion was a function of ideology. Its jurisprudential exponents presumed it to be correct, but they never really bothered to explain in a persuasive fashion why it should have constitutional status. Economic liberty as presented had no obvious linkage to the Fourteenth Amendment's central reason for existence which, as the separate but equal doctrine's emergence demonstrated, largely had been forgotten anyway. Redirection of the Fourteenth Amendment, necessitating the importation of new values and engraftment of principle, did not constitute a serious dereliction as a matter of general process. Judicial review was remiss and antidemocratic because it reflected no sensitivity toward or consultation of society's evolving ways. Such disregard was evidenced by the Court's conclusory rather than expository pronouncements.

Chief Justice Marshall's work is susceptible to portrayal as partisan and ideological, but it nonetheless was characterized by a palpable commitment to explication betokening a sense of account-ability and implying that principle could not stand if the public was not persuaded of its necessity and propriety. In contrast, Loch-nerism from the outset was vulnerable to criticism for effectuating results which were convenient, rather than principles which were compelling, and impairing the emergence of what eventually would become a dominant viewpoint.[22] Apparent indifference to popular sentiment eventually would prove fatal to the principles which were propounded and almost lethal to the institution itself.

The Court in *Lochner* determined that state regulation of bakers' working hours breached an employer's and employee's freedom to contract.[23] To reach that decision, it was necessary to disregard or discount the unequal bargaining power between the contracting parties. The Court's fixation with its own dogma was evidenced by the crucial depiction of the regulation as labor legisla-tion "pure and simple," rather than as an exercise of the state's power to govern health and safety.[24] Unexpounded attachment of an exclusive label to an act or practice, when more than one fits, is a strong suggestion of result-oriented analysis. Such manipulation was too transparent, however, to disguise pursuit of a convenient result.[25] The subjectivism of the opinion was particularly oppro-brious because of its deceitful packaging. A majority professed ad-herence to principles of restraint, maintaining that it was not "sub-stituting the judgment of the Court for that of the legislature."[26] The sheerness of its claim and presumptive nature of its focus were revealed, however, by the further pronouncement that "We do not believe in the soundness of the views which uphold the law."[27]

The Court thus constitutionalized an increasingly dated and debated value system as a means of securing it against the normal processes of political and social reevaluation. Whatever grip social Darwinist concepts had upon the citizenry was far from comprehen-sive. Given the swelling volume of economic and social welfare legislation focusing upon the power and influence of private enter-prise, and terms of employment and conditions in the workplace, it was apparent that the ideology behind contractual liberty was increasingly controverted and perceptibly receding. In contrast to the more frequent concern of having the judiciary moving too far ahead of the citizenry, Lochnerism was a case of the Court's lagging behind and even impairing the effectuation of evolving societal values.

Even if the Court's persistent obstruction of state regulatory power evinced a sincere valuation of the role of economic freedom, the transformation into constitutional principle was referenced to chosen priorities without any evidence of considering societal inclinations. What is especially striking about that conversion is in just a few decades the Court had dismissed racial equality so completely from the Fourteenth Amendment's purview. If given even a fraction of the constitutional sympathy afforded private economic interests, the separate but equal doctrine would have had a more forceful demeanor.

In any event, Lochnerist thought is analytically distinguishable from an inquiry into values and identification of principle that strive to account persuasively for their existence. Although such analysis is not immune to manipulation, accountability enhances the likelihood of viable and durable results. The lessons of Lochnerism do not support an argument against value-based inquiry generally but cautions instead against constitutional lawmaking that does not take seriously the obligation to explain itself or monitor feedback.

When the Court seriously miscalculates or disregards popular sentiment, the legislature likely will work to reclaim lost ground. Contractual liberty notwithstanding, states continued to adopt regulations designed to govern conditions in the workplace. Although subject to constitutional suspicion, most legislation actually survived.[28] Vitality was attributable not only to the sheer volume of enactments, all of which could not possibly have been reviewed, but to the Court's own acknowledgment that liberty of contract was not absolute.[29]

Because the Court's professed concern was with regulation that exceeded state powers and was unconnected to a legitimate purpose,[30] a practical response was to fortify legislative records to demonstrate convincingly that challenged enactments promoted a valid interest. Detailed evidentiary presentations of a health or safety problem thus convinced the Court sometimes that an enactment represented a valid exercise of a state's police power.[31] Deferral of contractual freedom in such instances, however, sometimes was a function of superseding values no less presumptive than those displaced.

Marketplace freedom first fell not to deliberative consultation of competing values but to prevalent gender stereotypes. Regulation of working hours for women was upheld pursuant to the Court's articulated concerns with their physical weakness, traditional dependence upon men, inherent disabilities and disadvantages and other inferiorities.[32] The decision was no less conclusory in tone than previous assertions that liberty of contract was a fundamental right. It essentially represented a triumph of assumption over assumption, rather than the operation of values and principles that were convincingly expounded.

In enunciating and advancing marketplace freedom as constitutional edict, the Court dismissed some well-established principles that proved inconvenient. Chief Justice Marshall in the early Nineteenth Century had declared that Congress' power to regulate commerce was not limited to just "traffic."[33] Federal regulation of wage, hour and workplace conditions, which paralleled state initiatives and further reflected the influence of societal values snubbed by the Court, was not inconsistent with Marshall's broad delineation of the commerce power. The Court, however, adopted a reading of the commerce clause that was as cramped as interpretation of the Fourteenth Amendment had been expansive. By tooling the due process clause into an instrument of economic liberty, the Court blunted a broad range of state social and economic reform. Its recasting of the commerce clause sentenced federal initiatives to a like fate.

By construing the commerce power narrowly, so that it primarily related to the movement rather than manufacture of goods, the Court invalidated much federal regulation of industry and labor. Standards of employment that directly concerned the safety or efficiency of railroad traffic survived, for instance, because they more palpably related to the movement of commerce.[34] The Court characterized federally mandated pension plans for railroad employees as a social welfare rather than commerce concern and invalidated them.[35] Federal child labor legislation, prohibiting interstate transport of goods produced with the help of underage employees, also was declared beyond the scope of the commerce power.[36]

Absent proof that an activity directly if not exclusively implicated the distribution process, regulation would be invalidated as an unconstitutional infringement upon manufacturing and private enterprise. The consequent points of distinction were interstate transportation, over which Congress had authority, and production, which was a matter for local regulation.[37] The Court's observation that maintenance of state authority "over matters purely local . . . [was] essential to the preservation of our institutions,"[38] however, seemed almost cynical in its failure to notice the impediments it had erected to such regulation in the name of contractual liberty.

Importation of values without a meaningful survey of the citizenry's bearings, or commitment to accounting for resultant constitutional embellishment, was an affront to democratic expectations and properly subject to condemnation from its inception. What made the Court even more subject to opproprium was its tenacious adherence to marketplace priorities as the nation plunged into economic depression and increasingly expressed its preference for a different set of values. While other branches of government sought to formulate policies reflecting newer visions and ideology, the Court remained locked in its doctrinal ways and impeded governmental initiative.

The increasingly manifest need for a coordinated national response to deteriorating social and economic conditions underscored the perspicacity of Chief Justice Marshall's original broad reading of the commerce power. Incapacity of the states to fashion and orchestrate a national recovery program illustrated the need for a broad commerce power as clearly as early trade friction among the states had demonstrated it to Marshall. The Court, however, regarded New Deal policies as a particularly insidious assault upon free enterprise principles. Consequently, it dismissed President Roosevelt's restorative initiatives in wholesale fashion and further tightened its grip upon national economic policy. Adhering rigidly to its notion that commerce pertained solely to the process of distribution, the Court invalidated wage, price and hour controls.[39] An inflexibly narrow definition of commerce also refused to admit agricultural production, manufacturing processes and working conditions within its purview.[40] Consistently, the Court resisted the notion that certain productive activities might be sufficiently related to commerce so "that for the protection of the one there is the need to regulate the other."[41] Instead, it insisted that economic recovery must be accomplished consistent with the constitution, and "Extraordinary conditions do not create or enlarge constitutional power."[42]

By intimating that its pronouncements were emitted from within the walls of the constitution, instead of judicially transported there, the Court obscured the true nature of its review. In reality, the judiciary had become mired in a political debate over governing values and set in a position from which it refused to budge. If the constitution truly spoke on behalf of the Court's position, such intractability would have been understandable. Because the values it selected to activate the constitution were a product of discretion, however, the Court's obduracy and insensitivity to societal predilections proved especially grievous.

Fueled by a strong popular mandate to pursue economic reform in his second term, Roosevelt confronted the judiciary's intransigence with a plan that challenged the institution's structure and function. Contemplating a more sympathetic forum for his agenda, Roosevelt proposed the appointment of an additional justice for each member who was at least seventy years old and had served a minimum of ten years.[43] If implemented, the scheme immediately would have increased the number of justices to fifteen, with a majority favorably disposed toward New Deal reforms.[44] Although Congress defeated the obvious challenge to the Court's authority,[45]

Roosevelt's objectives were swiftly realized anyway. Whether or not bending to stepped up political pressure, the Court expanded its reading of the commerce power, deferred to legislative judgment on economic and social welfare policy and finally surrendered its guardianship of economic liberty.[46] Within the next few years, because of death or retirement, Roosevelt was able to fill eight vacancies and thereby clear away three decades worth of judicial obstruction to marketplace regulation.[47]

The reorganization plan has been depicted as the most serious threat ever to the Court's authority and its role as a neutral arbiter of constitutional issues.[48] Such a characterization is exaggerated. Roosevelt's reaction was a legitimate exercise by a coordinate branch of government which, in a dynamic framework of separation of powers, merely adjusted malleable dividing lines of authority to meet pragmatic and pertinent ends of governance. The overtly political nature of his strategy may account for the negative perceptions of it. The Court, however, had been at least as political for the preceding three decades. In the process, it lost sight of the fact that it was a medium not through which the constitution revealed its meaning but through which it passed values to actuate the document. Because those values were borrowed from outside the constitution itself, the Court in a democratic society had an accounting duty which it failed to perform. Given a judiciary which thusly misconceived or forgot its role, the Court set its own self up for a harsh reawakening to its responsibilities.

The *Lochner* era revealed a judiciary with a distorted sense of the constitution and itself. Principles formulated from external values were not connected to dominant societal concerns. Instead of offering a convincing reason for their selection and operation, the Court attributed them to constitutional ordination. Such review suggests an institution that may be dedicated to the culture of the law but is detached from the culture of the people. Confusion of value discernment and doctrinal engraftment with documental exactment facilitates a sense of infallibility that in turn diminishes awareness of the need for reflection, explanation and sometimes revision. An institutional mind set of that nature poses an undeniably significant threat to democratic principles. Unabating regulatory initiatives in spite of hostile constitutional pronouncements should have notified the Court of the need at least to reexamine the values behind the principles it was crafting. Political buffeting and even bullying, in a society that contemplates effective mechanisms for controlling the exercise of power, were fitting responses to judicial disregard of the imperatives conditioning the exercise of its power. Given the Court's ways, the most apt criticism of Roosevelt's plan may be that it was belated.

Misdirected as the Court may have been in its function, the lessons from that chapter in jurisprudential history have been exaggerated and misunderstood. Construction of the right of privacy, for instance, reflexively has been criticized as Lochnerist. Such a description is apt only insofar as both privacy and contractual liberty are principles derived from external values and engrafted upon the constitution. The right of privacy, however, was crafted with attention to values that obviously permeated society. Although still pretending that the constitution was speaking for itself, the Court tendered an explanation for the principle that was lucid and persuasive. Such accountability and consequent public acclaim ensured general survival of the notion and established its compatibility with democratic expectations. Even if less arguably tied to constitutional text or design, a right of privacy strikes a more positive chord in a broad cross-section of the populace than contractual liberty as jurisprudentially framed ever did.

Although seldom willing to acknowledge it and inclined at times to obscure its enunciations as purported penumbras, emanations or implications of constitutional text or design, the Court since the demise of Lochnerism has not sworn off value importation. Perhaps to remind of if not guarantee against the vices of Lochnerism, modern cultivation of constitutional liberty focuses upon what is "implicit in the concept of ordered liberty" or "rooted in the nation's conscience and traditions."[49] Such an inquiry probably minimizes the likelihood that the Court would enunciate a constitutional principle not subscribed to by a substantial segment of the citizenry. At minimum, it requires the judiciary to concentrate upon public perceptions of what the constitution can support and what the citizenry itself will countenance.

Theoretically, the values from which the Court might fashion principle are infinite. Unless insensitive to democratic interests and willing to have its convictions worn down by incessant popular and legislative challenges, the Court is unlikely to engraft a requirement upon the constitution without reckoning first with whether the citizenry subscribes to or eventually may invest in its premises.

It is not necessarily symptomatic of Lochnerism if the Court stands upon principles and puts into effect values about which are significantly controverted. Refusal to retreat from the desegregation mandate for nearly two decades, despite fierce resistance from and evasion by state and local officials, is a prominent example of justifiable perseverance. Opposition to the desegregation mandate could be and was expressed in terms that the Court disregarded deeply held values tied to custom and tradition and even abridged "something that can be called a 'freedom of the white.'"[50] The dismantling of official segregation, however, cannot be lumped with insistence upon marketplace freedom under the category of democratically inconsonant review. The Court's search for enlightened and durable values as a preface to its desegregation order was manifest.

Explication and accountability, which was missing altogether in *Lochner* and its progeny, was especially abundant in *Brown* and its successors. Assignment of enforcement state and local officials and the eventual emergence of significant limiting principles, moreover, reflected sensitivity and responsiveness to the imperatives of democratic consent. A significant distinction between *Brown* and *Lochner*, therefore, was the identification of values and expoundment of principles in a convincing fashion rather than from a presumptive and unexplicated set of priorities. Three decades after the desegregation mandate, *Brown* is commonly adverted to in reverent tones. The *Lochner* decision even now is assailed as an aberration if not abomination.

Reference to external values supported by resulting principles affords no absolute assurance that constitutional law will escape distortion. Presumably, any idiosyncratic preference can be expounded upon in elegant terms and attributed to a collective rather than individual conscience. The appellation of "family values", as noted previously, is sufficiently malleable to support competing concepts of constitutionality that may or may not have significant societal support.[51] Similarly susceptible to manipulation is the notion of "color-blindness," which has been alluded to both in upholding and invalidating affirmative action concepts.[52] Even if the potential exists for antidemocratic excursions, the need for externally referenced constitutional principles remains invariable.

Failure to construct and engraft fundamental principles from imported values ensures constitutional torpor. It has been when external but pertinent values were entirely or mostly untapped, as evidenced by slavery, segregation and other variants of oppression, that the consequences of judicial review have been most objectionable. Value selection and infusion is essential if any practical sense is to be made of and service derived from the constitution. Without that process of choice and application, "equal protection of the laws"[53] for instance would be an amorphous and impotent statement instead of a proscription against race, sex or other variants of discrimination.

Reference of law to outside value is standard methodology even for those who habitually denounce it, yet conclude that a superficially undifferentiating "freedom of speech clause"[54] does not protect all types of expression. The protection of some but not other forms of expression is a function not of explicit constitutional command but engrafted meaning.[55] A determination that street vernacular is unfit for broadcast and thus constitutionally unprotected,[56] for instance, reflects nothing more than a choice of values unrelated to actual terms of the constitution. Justifications for such line-drawing, which as discussed in the next chapter is a common practice, may refer to constitutional design or implication. If so, these justifications too hide from the reality that the constitution does not announce values but merely responds to those attached to it.

Obfuscation of the nature and needs of the process accounts for

the hypocrisy of some modern criticism that depicts the Court's validation of slavery as "derelict"[57] and as a perverse constitutional
result. Although the opinion is more than a century old and
thoroughly disgraced, it is not an apt reference point for objecting
to modern jurisprudence referenced to outside values. The fact is
that neither a due process nor equal protection clause existed to guide
the Court's thinking then. Modern criticism, moreover, cannot discount the dominant societal values of the time that were consonant
with rather than crossed by the jurisprudential sentiments expressed.

The possibility that the judiciary will operate as defiantly as it
did in negating popular sentiment and legislative output earlier this
century is lessened to the extent that Lochnerism is remembered in
a profoundly negative way. The mere mention of contractual liberty continues to arouse institutional palpitations and unhappy
constitutional memories. Disclamation of Lochnerism is a common
if not reflexive chant of modern Fourteenth Amendment analysis.
The Court routinely denounces Lochnerism in refusing to probe
legislative judgment on economic matters and even as a preface to
constructing other fundamental rights from outside values.[58] The
era of Lochnerism officially concluded in 1938.[59] Continuing
references to the vices associated with it evidence the still powerful
grip the experience has on the nation's jurisprudence.

Preoccupation with and criticism of Lochnerism remains so
embedded in the legal culture that jurists probably are conditioned
to be careful rather than adventurous. The Court's retreat from
contractual liberty accelerated as President Roosevelt reconstituted
the Court and memories of the *Lochner* era were passed on. In the
*Lochner* case itself, Justice Holmes had dissented on grounds that
constitutional principle was merely an extension of "Mr. Herbert
Spencer's Social [Darwinism] theories."[60] Upon finally rejecting
Lochnerism, the Court observed that whether "the legislature takes
for its textbook Adam Smith, Herbert Spencer, Lord Keynes or
some other is no concern of ours."[61]

Mistaken as the Court may have been in its selection of
values, the response of subsequent generations probably has been
exaggerated. Over the past half century, the Court only once has

invalidated state economic regulation as a violation of the Fourteenth Amendment.[62] Even then, it subsequently, uniformly and
emphatically overturned the decision and characterized it as an
aberration.[63] Instead of closely scrutinizing the means or ends of
economic policy, the Court now employs a "rational basis test" that
essentially translates into consideration of whether any conceivable
reason would justify the government's action. It is a standard
overtly calibrated against disrupting representative governance and
effectuates in reality what for the *Lochner* Court was a pretense.
Such extreme deference reflects a lesson drawn by the judiciary
itself "that the constitution...can actively intrude into...eco-
nomic and policy matters only if...prepared to bear enormous
institutional and social costs."[64]

Willingness to conceive of justifications for a singular class of
legislative action presumes that the main fault of Lochnerism was
closely reviewing a particular category of regulation. Such a conclusion disregards the inevitability that important societal interests
may be touched in any area where the legislature acts. Absent that
recognition, a facet of the legislative process may be immune to constitutional standards and insulated from traditional checks and
balances promoting governmental fitness and quality. Justice
Powell noted that significant concerns can be neglected or impaired
if congressional oversight is compounded by judicial inattention.[65]
To ascertain whether the consequences of legislative action at least
were intended requires not a reversion to Lochnerism but at least
some modicum of review beyond "tautological recognition of the
fact that Congress did what it intended to do."[66]

Even a more probing inquiry into possible encroachments upon
liberty need not be mistaken as a repetition of past mistakes. In
upholding a state law requiring employers to give workers a half day
off so they could vote, the Court reiterated its reluctance to "sit as
a super-legislature" and referred to the measure as a routine business
regulation.[67] The characterization of the statute showed a judiciary
so steeped in the vices of Lochnerism that it was disabled from fully
appreciating or depicting the rather extortionate nature of the
provision.

To avoid the true sins of Lochnerism, the Court need not block out an entire category of law from its purview. In the event it intervenes, however, it must be prepared to provide a satisfying reason for doing so and make a convincing display of accountability. Forces in both the public and private sector would remain free to alter the citizenry's perception of a decision's desirability and legitimacy. Pending their possible success, any consequences of judicial review are fully consonant with democratic ways.

An astute understanding of Lochnerism should include recognition that the Court's delineation of liberty represented an exploration of largely uncharted constitutional territory. Inaugural ventures in discerning values and fashioning principle have not always produced the immediate brilliance often attributed to Chief Justice Marshall. Early interpretation of the equal protection and due process clauses respectively yielded the separate but equal doctrine and renderings that lacked a clear relationship to overarching purpose.[68] Initial readings of the First Amendment were so cramped that convictions for political dissent were the norm rather than the exception.[69] The clear and present danger test, which today protects political expression unless the risks it presents are real, substantial and imminent,[70] at first operated against perceived evils that were vague, imagined and remote. Nor are fitful starts in governance unique to the judiciary, as evidenced by delayed recognition that states as well as the federal government may be a threat to liberty.

The constitution itself emerged in response to a deficient and failing political structure. The nation's foundering under the Articles of Confederation, when the separate states consistently worked against rather than with one another, testifies further that original governmental craftings are likely to be inauspicious rather than flawless. The history of such miscalculations and improvements that followed, however, suggest that future decisions learn from past mistakes. Formative deficiencies thus constitute an argument for rather than against further initiative in selecting values and constructing principles.

Criticism of the judiciary's exercise of power during the *Lochner* era also obscures some meaningful accomplishments by a Court which, in attempting to develop the meaning of a liberty provision that is neither self-defining nor self-executing, begot constitutional law that has endured. Despite its faults, the *Lochner* era receives less credit than it deserves for the contributions it made to what are now, but were not then, commonly accepted concepts of liberty. Contemporary expressive freedoms and rights of the accused, for instance, are indebted to the seminal work of the same institution which propagated liberty of contract.[71] It was during the *Lochner* period that concepts of liberty were expanded beyond narrow common law notions to include:

> freedom from bodily restraint, ... the right of the individual to contract, to engage in any of the common occupations of life, to acquire useful knowledge, to marry, to establish a home and bring up children, to worship God according to the dictates of conscience, and generally to enjoy those privileges long recognized... as essential to the orderly pursuit of happiness by free men.[72]

Modern fundamental rights analysis, which has constitutionalized privacy, family, marriage, voting, travel and other basic but textually unenumerated interests, owes much to that rendition of Fourteenth Amendment liberty.[73] Examined from a broader perspective, early substantive due process review was not an unqualified mistake, and in fact constituted a starting point for significant constitutional progress.

The positive legacy of the *Lochner* era does not obscure or minimize the real distortion that occurred in the judicial process and in constitutional law. Those perversions ultimately do not, however, afford a compelling case against the continuing importation of values to develop fundamental principles. Judicial review like any other governmental process is subject to checking influences which, as discussed in the next chapter, are diverse and effective. If Lochnerism represents the worst danger connected with value importation, more cause exists for reassurance than distress. Lochnerism and other ill-fated constitutional ventures instruct that if the Court becomes too aloof or intransigent, it risks political conflict from which it inevitably will emerge as a loser. That reality was understood by Chief Justice Marshall, who knew Jefferson would ignore any order to deliver Marbury's commission. It was acted upon by President Roosevelt, who styled his reorganizational maneuverings as a plan to save the "Constitution from hardening of the judicial arteries."[74] The lesson remains prominent in the modern Court's mind, as evidenced by its continuing refusal even to contemplate concepts of economic liberty and visible obsession with choosing values that will be broadly and readily endorsed.

It is normatively assumed, unless demonstrated otherwise, that those who govern generally exercise their responsibility in good faith. Although that supposition does not preclude criticism or even cynicism toward performance of official responsibility, its absence is subversive of effective representative governance. Over-reaction to the Court's capacity to abuse power may deny the judiciary and society an essential benefit of the doubt and, in so doing, diminish both the institution and the constitution. Instances of dereliction are an immutable part of the Court's history, but those deviations or the potential of future abuse should not be exaggerated or excessively determinative of the judiciary's function. The risk that some principles may be perverted is a danger of having any principles at all.

# References

1. *Moore v. City of East Cleveland*, 431 U.S. 494, 503–04 (1977).

2. *Id.* at 544 (White, J., dissenting).

3. *See* Brownstein, *With or Without Supreme Court Changes, Reagan Will Reshape the Federal Bench*, 49 NAT'L L.J. 2338, 2340 (1984).

4. *Webster v. Reproductive Health Service*, 109 S.Ct. 3040 (1989).

5. *Bowers v. Hardwick*, 478 U.S. 186, 194 (1986).

6. *See id.* at 191–195.

7. *See, e.g., Roe v. Wade*, 410 U.S. 113 (1973) (privacy includes freedom to elect abortion; *Eisenstadt v. Baird*, 405 U.S. 438, (1972) (privacy safeguards rights of individuals to procreate or use contraceptives).

8. *Bowers v. Hardwick*, 478 U.S. at 191.

9. *See id.* at 194–95.

10. The Court in the past has demonstrated the independence of privacy as a constitutional interest by disallowing prosecution for possession of obscene materials in one's home, even though sale or distribution was unlawful. *Stanley v. Georgia*, 394 U.S. 557 (1969).

11. *See, e.g., Bowers v. Hardwick*, 478 U.S. at 194–95.

12. Moments when the Court has been visibly most activist sometimes have been accompanied by explicit professions of denial. *See, e.g., infra* notes 24–25 and accompanying text.

13. 198 U.S. 45 (1905).

14. *See, e.g., Zablocki v. Redhail*, 434 U.S. 374, 407 (1978) (Rehnquist, J., dissenting) (right of marriage); *Vlandis v. Kline*, 412 U.S. 449 (1973) (Rehnquist, J., dissenting) (right to travel), *Griswold v. Connecticut*, 381 U.S. 479, 507–08 (1965) (Black, J., dissenting) (right of privacy).

15. U.S. CONST., art. I, §10.

16. *See Allgeyer v. Louisiana*, 165 U.S. 578 (1897); *Mugler v. Kansas*, 123 U.S. 623 (1887); *Munn v. Illinois*, 94 U.S. 113 (1877).

17. *See Griswold v. Connecticut*, 381 U.S. at 481–85.

18. U.S. CONST., amend. XIV.

19. *See Brown v. Board of Education*, 347 U.S. 483, 490 (1954): L. TRIBE, GOD SAVE THIS HONORABLE COURT 46 (1986).

20. *See* A.T. MASON, WILLIAM HOWARD TAFT – CHIEF JUSTICE 157–58 (1983).

21. *See id.*

22. *Lochner v. New York*, 198 U.S. 45, at 75 (Holmes, J., dissenting).

23. *Id.* at 61–64.

24. *Id.* at 57.

25. Justice Holmes noted from the outset that progressive social forces were being held hostage to a chosen social philosophy. *See Lochner v. New York*, 198 U.S. at 75 (Holmes, J., dissenting).

26. *Id.* at 56–57.

27. *Id.* at 61.

28. *See* G. GUNTHER, CONSTITUTIONAL LAW 453–54 (1985).

29. *Lochner v. New York*, 198 U.S. at 63.

30. *See, e.g., Lochner v. New York*, 198 U.S. at 57.

31. Fact-filled submissions to the Court eventually became known as "Brandeis briefs," in honor of the success of Louis Brandeis' successful efforts in *Muller v. Oregon*, 208 U.S. 412 (1908).

32. *Id.* at 421–23.

33. *See Gibbons v. Ogden*, 22 U.S. (9 Wheat.) 1, 189–96 (1824).

34. *E.g., Baltimore and Ohio Railway v. Interstate Commerce Commission*, 221 U.S. 612 (1911).

35. *Railroad Retirement Board v. Alton Railroad Company* 295 U.S. 330 (1935).

36. *Hammer v. Dagenhart* 247 U.S. 251 (1918).

37. *Id.* at 271–72.

38. *Id.* at 275.

39. *See Schecter Poultry Corporation v. United States*, 295 U.S. 495 (1935).

40. *See, e.g. Carter v. Carter Coal Company*, 298 U.S. 238, 304 (1936); *United States v. Butler*, 297 U.S. 1, 73 (1936).

41. 298 U.S. at 327 (Cardozo, J., dissenting).

42. *Schecter Poultry Corporation v. United States*, 295 U.S. at 528.

43. *See* H. ABRAHAM, JUSTICES AND PRESIDENTS 292–93 (1974).
44. *See id.*
45. *See id.*
46. *See, e.g., National Labor Relations Board v. Jones and Laughlin Steel Corporation,* 301 U.S. 1 (1937); *West Coast Hotel Company v. Parrish,* 300 U.S. 379 (1937).
47. *See* L. TRIBE, supra note 19, at 34, 90–91; L. PFEFFER, THIS HONORABLE COURT 317–21 (1965).
48. *See, e.g.,* J. NOWAK, R. ROTUNDA & J. YOUNG, CONSTITUTIONAL LAW, §11.3, at 348 (1986).
49. *See, e.g., Zablocki v. Redhail,* 434 U.S. at 383–84 (marriage); *Moore v. City of East Cleveland* 431 U.S. at 503–04 (family); *Roe v. Wade* 410 U.S. at 152 (privacy).
50. Black, *The Lawfulness of the Desegregation Decisions,* 69 YALE L.J. 421, 429 (1960).
51. *See supra* notes 1–3 and accompanying text.
52. *See City of Richmond v. J.A. Croson Company,* 109 S.Ct. 706, 720–21 (1989) (racial preferences contravene a color-blind constitution); *Regents of the University of California v. Bakke,* 438 U.S. 265, 407 (1978) (Blackmun, J., concurring and dissenting).
53. U.S. CONST., amend. XIV.
54. U.S. CONST., amend. I.
55. Pursuant to the externally created but not consensually subscribed to theory that speech pertaining to self-government is most valuable, the Court has afforded political expression utmost constitutional protection. *See Central Hudson Gas & Electric Company v. Public Service Commission,* 447 U.S. 557, 561–63 (1980); 579–83 (Stevens, J., concurring); 595–99 (Rehnquist, J., dissenting). Expression, if denominated as commercial or defamatory is less protected and, if classified as obscene or fighting words, is entirely unprotected. *See id.* (commercial speech); *New York Times Company v. Sullivan,* 376 U.S. 254 (1964), (defamation); *Roth v. United States* 354 U.S. 476 (1957) (obscenity); *Chaplinsky v. New Hampshire,* 315 U.S. 568 (1942) (fighting words).
56. *See FCC v. Pacifica Foundation,* 438 U.S. 726 (1978).
57. Meese III, *The Law of the Constitution* 61 Tulane L. REV. 979, 989 (1987).
58. The Court thus has observed that the "judiciary may not sit as a superlegislature judging the wisdom of" economic policy, *New Orleans v. Dukes,* 427 U.S. 297, 303 (1976). In developing the right of privacy, the Court nonetheless adverted to "Mr. Justice Holmes' admonition in his now-vindicated dissent in Lochner." *Roe v. Wade,* 410 U.S. at 117.
59. Thereafter, the Court would refuse to find economic regulation unconstitutional unless it would "preclude the assumption that it rests upon some rational basis." *United States v. Carolene Products,* 304 U.S. 144, 152–53 (1938).
60. *Lochner v. New York,* 198 U.S. at 75 (Holmes, J., dissenting).
61. *Ferguson v. Skrupa,* 372 U.S. 726, 732 (1963).
62. *Morey v. Doud,* 354 U.S. 457 (1957).
63. *City of New Orleans v. Dukes,* 427 U.S. at 306.
64. *United States Trust Company v. New Jersey,* 431 U.S. 1, 62 (1978) (Brennan, J., dissenting).

65. *Schweiker v. Wilson*, 450 U.S. 221, 247 (1981) (Powell, J., dissenting).
66. *United States Railroad Retirement Board v. Fritz*, 449 U.S. 166, 180 (1980) (Stevens, J., concurring).
67. *Day-Brite Lighting, Inc. v. Missouri*, 342 U.S. 421, 425 (1952).
68. See *Plessy v. Ferguson*, 163 U.S. 537 (1896) (enunciating separate but equal doctrines); *Lochner v New York*, 198 U.S. 45 (economic liberty upon Fourteenth Amendment).
69. See *Whitney v. California*, 274 U.S. 357 (1927); *Gitlow v. New York*, 268 U.S. 652 (1925); *Abrams v. United States*, 250 U.S. 616 (1919); *Debs v. United States*, 249 U.S. 211 (1919); *Schenck v. United States*, 249 U.S. 47 (1919).
70. See *Brandenburg v. Ohio*, 395 U.S. 444, 447–49 (1969).
71. See, e.g., *Powell v. Alabama*, 287 U.S. 45, 68–71 (1932) (right to counsel essential to due process); *Near v. Minnesota*, 238 U.S. 697, 713 (1931) (First Amendment forbids prior restraint).
72. *Meyer v. Nebraska*, 262 U.S. 625, 626 (1923).
73. See, e.g., *Moore v. City of East Cleveland*, 431 U.S. at 502.
74. Radio Address by President Roosevelt (March 9, 1937).

## Six

# Gravitational Realities
# of a Democratic Society

Lost too often amidst the din of competing theories of judicial review is the reality that the institution functions within a system of checks and balances that largely are effective in harnessing and sometimes even enslaving it to popular sentiment. The fact that jurisprudence consistently has been inspired by sensitivity and responsiveness to majoritarian interests is unfortunate for critics whose theories thereby lose any practical urgency. It is a reality that accounts well, however, for the imperative that official action must be consented to by the governed. Given the Court's sensitivities and performance, detractors should be reassured rather than distressed by the overall nature and operation of judicial review. The caution and conservatism characterizing modern delineation of fundamental rights, for instance, represents a jurisprudential norm rather than exception. Even decisions which are reflexively and retrospectively condemned, such as those endorsing slavery or constructing the separate but equal doctrine, did not stray significantly from dominant sentiments of their time. The regularity with which judicially chosen values and consequent principles reflect majoritarian sensitivities should not be surprising insofar as mainstream referenced political institutions tend to select jurists from mainstream culture.

Consequent steerage of law toward a common political denominator is regularly evidenced when the Court is called upon to vitalize the constitution. First Amendment jurisprudence which

125

refuses to protect expression that is purportedly indecent or offensive is primarily a function of orthodox sensitivities.[1] So too is a decision which permits display of a nativity scene on public property and overlooks the official favoritism toward Christianity.[2] A failure to discern discriminatory intent, when a Southern city only recently governed by segregation erected a traffic wall between a white and black neighborhood, likewise reflects a tilt toward dominant culture.[3] Such results have been faulted for reflecting an "acute ethnocentric myopia ... and depressing inability to appreciate that in our land of cultural pluralism, there are many who think, act, and talk differently from the Members of [the] Court, and who do not share their ... sensibilities."[4] Insensitive as they may be toward cultural diversity, the decisions plainly are not the work of an institution at odds with popular sentiment or inclination.

Modern Fourteenth Amendment analysis, although hypersensitive to the lessons of Lochnerism, nonetheless has not refrained entirely from expounding the meaning of liberty. Contemporary embellishment of the Fourteenth Amendment is most notable for its highly conservative nature. The Court, for instance, has rejected arguments for elevating personal lifestyle or grooming preferences[5] and homosexuality[6] to a level of constitutional concern, even though they could be persuasively justified as legitimate autonomy or traditional privacy interests. In ordering desegregation of public schools, the Court characterized education as "perhaps the most important function of state and local governments," described educational opportunity as central to "the performance of our most basic public responsibilities ... [and as] the very foundation of good citizenship," and concluded "it is doubtful that any child may reasonably be expected to succeed in life if he is denied the opportunity of an education."[7] Despite also referring to education as a liberty that cannot be arbitrarily deprived,[8] the Court nonetheless refrained from declaring it a fundamental right.[9]

The Court rightly has observed that "history counsels caution and restraint.... But it does not counsel abandonment."[10] In equally lucid moments, it has noted that the potential for abuse swells when "judicial intervention becomes [determined by] the predilections of those who happen at the time to be Members of this Court."[11] What it has been reluctant to acknowledge out loud, and maybe to itself, is a central responsibility for choosing values from a virtually limitless moral universe. The profoundly negative imagery of Lochnerism probably makes a candid pronouncement of its role impolitic. What tends to follow as a consequence are references to penumbras, implications of ordered liberty and other concepts purportedly drawn from documentary text or design. In reality, they merely divert attention from the Court's selection and setting of priorities.

Modern fundamental rights analysis is distinguished by a reluctance to substantively animate the Fourteenth Amendment. It also reflects an overt commitment to searching out values largely subscribed to by the citizenry and awareness of the need to furnish compelling reasons for its conclusions. In reaction to the condemnation of Lochnerism, contemporary inquiry focuses upon whether an interest is "implicit in a concept of ordered liberty" or "rooted in the nation's conscience and values."[12] It may be true that "what the deeply rooted traditions of the country are is arguable; [and] which of them deserves the protection on the Due Process Clause is even more debatable."[13] Such an inquiry, even if not entirely immune from subjective manipulation, nonetheless benefits both the judiciary and the public. It forces the Court to establish and maintain a dialogue with the citizenry in which it explicates the reasons for its conclusions and demonstrates why the values it discerns and principles it enunciates merit constitutional status. Such review betokens the accountability missing in Lochnerism and largely responsible for its bad name.

The process of charting fundamental rights derived from outside values in a practical sense commences as an official moral statement that becomes a settled principle only when broadly acclaimed by the citizenry. A conscientious effort to ascertain whether a principle is implicit in ordered liberty concepts or supported by the nation's values requires a sensitive examination of societal history, traditions and expectations and satisfactory display that such an appraisal has been performed. As noted before, the formula is not magical or immune to perversion. It is difficult, however, to market as a commonly held value what only has limited circulation or subscription and thus permanently obscure what is actually a matter of idiosyncratic preference. The entire Lochnerist legacy demonstrates how failure to grasp that imperative breeds principle with poor prospects for long-term survival.[14]

No aspect of contemporary fundamental rights analysis has been more evocative of dissonance than the decision to include abortion within the right of privacy. In *Roe v. Wade*,[15] the Court declared that a women may choose an abortion as a matter of her own discretion during the first three months of pregnancy.[16] It also determined that her liberty interest over the next three months was subject to qualification only for purposes of ensuring her health and safety.[17] Only during the third trimester, when the Court recognizes a state interest in potential life, may abortion be prohibited and then only if the mother's life and health is not endangered.[18]

From the moment that it recognized the right to elect an abortion as a constitutional liberty interest, the Court has been chastised for disregarding its own criteria for identification of fundamental liberties. Because most states had restricted abortion for at least a century, it was argued that freedom of choice was not rooted deeply enough in the nation's traditions and values to be of constitutional striping.[19] Public opinion since the decision, however, has remained constant and especially supportive of its practicalities. A large majority of the citizenry favors freedom of choice if the mother's health or life would be endangered, if the pregnancy is the result of rape or if abortion is performed during the first trimester.[20] A small minority opposes abortion for any reason.[21] Insofar as the vast number of abortions are performed within the initial three months of pregnancy, the pragmatics of the decision seem well-attuned to dominant preferences.

Raw public sentiment in no event can be the exclusive determinant of constitutional principle. If it were, issues such as slavery, segregation and First Amendment freedoms could be decided by a plebiscite, and constitutional contours would be an exclusive function of time, region and emotion minus any pretense of governance by a higher standard. To the extent that the Court identifies traditions and values rooted in the nation's conscience, and ultimately must convince the citizenry of the wisdom of its choice, popular inclinations nonetheless are pertinent. Given a public divided not so much over the existence but the scope of the liberty, the freedom could be delineated more narrowly and still be consonant with societal norms. Because of the timing of most abortions, definition of the right congruent with circumstances in which abortion as an option is broadly supported would have little practical consequence.

The original charting of abortion rights nonetheless has been derided as more dangerous than *Lochner* and its progeny, because the latter at least "did us the favor of sowing the seeds of their own destruction."[22] Elevation of abortion to a constitutional status also has been depicted as a raw exercise of judicial power declaring imperiously that the regulatory "goal is not important enough to sustain the restriction."[23] Even if legitimate arguments can be made that the Court stretched the right of privacy too far, characterization of the decision as neo–Lochnerist is hyperbolic. If truly a significant departure from widely held values, the right to elect an abortion would not be a durable principle.[24]

As the *Lochner* era demonstrated and subsequent generations of jurists seem to have learned especially well, enunciations unmet by widespread approval are unlikely to withstand the invariable challenges to their existence. Continuing legislative assaults upon the scope of abortion rights demonstrate that ultimate charting of the constitutional principle is still in progress and subject to democratic influence. The continuing epilogue to the abortion decision actually demonstrates effectively how any judicial pronouncement is not necessarily the final word but the beginning of an interaction among representative forces that ultimately determines constitutional configuration.

Legislative reaction not only has contested the wisdom of the Court's judgment but influenced the contouring of the right. Both federal and state prohibitions against public funding of abortion have been upheld,[25] as have certain notification requirements for minors.[26] The Court also has determined that a state may prohibit the performance of nontherapeutic abortions by public employees and in public facilities.[27] The jurisprudential record as it pertains to abortion thus is less evocative of rule by judicial fiat than of a continuing evolutionary process subject to the influence of representative forces. If not compelling enough in their present incarnation, the constitutional principles now governing abortion will have sowed the seeds of their own destruction too.

Notwithstanding the democratic gravitation of judicial review, modern commentary continues to thrive upon mischaracterization and misunderstanding. Jurisprudence that adverts to values not necessarily explicated or implicated by constitutional text thus remains subject to the aspersion that it is abusive of power. Typical of such misdirected and misleading criticism is Chief Justice Rehnquist's unremittingly sharp reprovals to the effect that the Court is reverting to Lochnerism when it activates the Fourteenth Amendment in a substantive fashion. Rehnquist has characterized the expansion of constitutional privacy to include abortion rights as a decision "closely attuned to . . . the majority opinion in *Lochner* and similar cases"[28] and declared recognition of rights to travel, to marry and of family to be of a similar ilk.[29] Such complaints are regularly accompanied by admonitions that the Court must limit its enunciations to what the document's text or design suggests.

When Rehnquist's own works are examined, it is not difficult to understand why all justices at one time or another are accused of being Lochnerist.[30] His reading of the equal protection clause as a bar to racial discrimination, including affirmative action and other preferential concepts that are remedial in nature, reflects principle derived from external value rather than from textual prescription or implication. Subscription to the notion that the intensity or review does not vary according to whether a law or action favors or burdens traditionally disadvantaged minorities[31] reflects a disputable vision of equal protection. It nonetheless is a conclusion of his own rather than the constitution's making and, as a value judgment, has no preordained priority over or immunity from the competing sense that race-conscious remedies are essential to get past racism.[32]

Determination that an equal protection violation cannot be established without a showing of discriminatory intent likewise is a controvertible product of value inspired constitutional embellishment rather than textual designation or structural intimation.[33] Its introduction by Rehnquist and others as a principle limiting the reach of equal protection further illustrates how the Court's enunciations do not suggest that the justices hear constitutional voices. A discriminatory intent standard is subject to the same criticism directed toward creation of abortion rights, insofar as it is cut from cloth of the Court's rather than the constitution's making.

Further reflective of constitutionally independent value judgment is Rehnquist's sense that gender classifications, unlike racial ones, should not be presumptively invalid.[34] The determination may be faithful to the Court's earliest equal protection rendition, which doubted that the provision ever would countenance a claim other than for race discrimination.[35] Even that holding left open the possibility, however, that a strong case might justify expansion of the guarantee beyond race.[36] Rehnquist's narrow reading in any event is not ordained by text and precedent but by his own intellectual processing of perceived relevancies which are entirely external to the constitution.

Reference to external values is even more conspicuous in Rehnquist's and the entire Court's ruminations concerning the meaning and reach of the First Amendment. On its face, "freedom of speech ... [and] of the press"[37] does not admit to qualification. Actual constitutional protection, however, has evolved from official selection among First Amendment philosophies and values rather than from inscribed right.[38] Rehnquist like other justices subscribes to the notion that political speech is the most worthy form of expression and thus entitled to highest constitutional regard.[39] The premise derives not from constitutional revelation but from Alexander Meiklejohn's theory that expression essential to informed self-government merits utmost First Amendment concern.[40]

Meiklejohn's ordering of speech priorities, however, is not without rivals. Competing doctrines, for instance, assess worth not from the perspective of what benefits society generally but what is useful for the individual. Alternative appraisals thus would afford utmost protection to expression, whether political or not, to the extent it facilitated self-development.[41] If adopted as a guide to First Amendment standards, such a reference point might support a higher constitutional premium upon nonpolitical speech variants including presently unprotected categories like obscenity and less protected forms such as commerical expression.

Rehnquist's diagramming of expressive freedom may be narrowly drawn but, like his delineations of liberty and equal protection, it is no less inspired by external values than chartings that would set broader constitutional perimeters. Classification reflecting valuation of speech has created a First Amendment hierarchy of protected, less protected and unprotected expression. Characterization of expression is an invariably treacherous and procrustean process. A political advertisement, for instance, may have dimensions that are both political and commercial. Rehnquist's depiction of such expression as commercial rather than political in nature[42] is reminiscent of the *Lochner* Court's determination that regulations in the workplace were purely labor and not health and safety enactments. In both instances, judgment not only may have been subjective but reflective of philosophical priority.

Even more clearly than the *Lochner* judgment, investment in a speech classification system demonstrates how constitutional enunciation routinely reflects an accumulation of value judgments merging into an ultimate pronouncement. The point is not that the Court should refrain from weaving constitutional fabric from its own thread, but that the process is unavoidable and should be honestly acknowledged. Image and substance would profit from an admission that constitutional law is largely a competition among values, the document does not speak or provide many hints about itself and no viewpoint is more sanctioned by the charter than another.

Despite the ubiquity and ineviability of value selection and effectuation, it seems much easier to condemn rather than confess to the true nature of the process. Justice Black, as noted in Chapter Two, consistently scolded the Court for deriving constitutional principle from outside values and regarded the notion of documental penumbras or emanations as a particularly insidious product of its imagination.[43] In joining an earlier decision recognizing freedom of association as a First Amendment interest,[44] however, he engaged in precisely the practice which he declared so objectionable.

Black may have regarded freedom of association, unlike the right of privacy, as an obvious implication of the First Amendment's announced terms. Any such conclusion mistakenly rests upon the premise that the constitution actively instructs when in reality it is passive unless the judiciary enlivens it. Freedom of association is necessary to activate freedom of expression, not because the constitution so specifies or implies, but because the Court understands the crucial nature of the relationship and insists upon it. Black's selective participation in the importation of values for constitutional purposes is a particularly graphic illustration of the tension existing between image and reality in the exercise of judicial power.

Black nonetheless allied himself with Judge Learned Hand's observation that "For myself it would be most irksome to be ruled by a bevy of Platonic Guardians, even if I knew how to choose them, which I assuredly do not."[45] Few would quibble with the proposition that judicial governance without accountability would be inimical to democratic ways and expectations. The equating of externally referenced constitutional law with Platonic elitism, however, is excessive. Plato regarded justice as a quality comprehensible only by wise philosophers who, as rulers of an ideal state, would provide enlightened but unquestioned governance.[46] A system of constitutional checks and balances designed to control all governmental power including judicial exercises of it, and one which anticipates public dissent from and disapproval of official judgment and action, is not the environment of absolute rule and societal docility contemplated by Plato.

133

A presumption that the Court has no higher claim to political wisdom has operated ever since the constitution's architects refused to vest it with a veto power.[47] Lochnerism may afford an example of institutional arrogance, but in the end it was a forceful reminder that the Court is not omniscient or beyond the reach of democratic influence. It is but one of many testaments to the imperative of judicial accountability to its clientele and the institution's dependence upon popular approval. Manifest from the Court's own history is the lesson that values, which do not connect well with popular perceptions of what the constitution should mean, provide a shaky foundation for enduring principles.

Because the ascertainment of fundamental values and consequent fashioning of principles are not always congruent with immediate public sentiment, the "Platonic Guardian" depiction at times may be superficially appealing. The characterization assumes, however, that the judiciary should be guided by the same forces of accountability to which the legislature may be subject. Seductive as it may be in a democratic system to defer to popular wisdom, the will of the public and engrafted will of the constitution need not always be correlative.[48] Value-based inquiry requires not just the relatively easy task of measuring public sentiment but the more complex assignment of discerning enduring or maturing tenets and convictions.

Tradition and conscience are dynamic entities which, as the demise of slavery, segregation and exclusive male rights and privileges demonstrates, are both evolutionary and devolutionary.[49] No measuring criteria are sensitive enough to detect precisely when a practice, way or belief commences or ceases to reflect a cardinal value. The fathoming of conscience in search of determinative ideals may be complicated by the presence of fear and anxiety, characteristic of the McCarthy age, or prejudice, common from the republic's founding. Ascertainment of values thus always runs the risk of being criticized as too regressive or too progressive.

Snapshot assessments of prevailing popular sentiments may afford scientific accuracy and an opportunity to tie constitutional principle to the immediate pulse of democracy. Such a process would be subject, however, to the danger of identifying reflexive attitudes, uninformed beliefs or tentative conclusions subject to the influence of fuller knowledge and further reflection. Both slavery and segregation proceeded with approval from a Court manifestly responsive to popular instinct. First Amendment rights if defined forever by common wisdom during the Red Scares of the 1920s or 1950s would be shadows of their present selves.

To avoid making the constitution a simple reflection of underdeveloped conception or preliminary bias, the Court's value judgments should be calibrated toward the expectations of an enlightened and reflective citizenry. It then becomes the Court's responsibility to complete the citizenry's education by explaining the reasons for the values it has chosen to effectuate. Failure to provide an accounting convincing enough to attract popular approval, as evidenced usually by unrelenting legislative challenge or disregard, indicates a judicial miscalculation. The standard of reference may be amorphous. It also may necessitate guesswork, beget erroneous conclusions and be seen as elitist. The risks are necessary, however, if constitutional principle is to be grounded in values that are sublime and enduring rather than ephemeral.

The disparity often noticeable between judicial words of restraint and deeds of activism may reflect the institution's own discomfort with an antidemocratic image. Discomfort with and divided sentiment regarding the judiciary's role are probably an inevitable function of the conflicting understandings and expectations to which the institution itself contributes. Such perplexity is reminiscent of the friction created by the emergence and operation of equity centuries ago.

Equity originally developed as a mechanism for ameliorating the sometimes harsh consequences of rigid common law and reflected a preference for issue resolution based upon fair play rather than legal fixation.[50] Its evolution bred tension between flexibility and certainty and concern for accountability.[51] A comparable stress exists in contemporary expectations that the Court must be faithful both to the demands of the constitution and representative governance. Worries that the necessary workings of judicial review pose a serious threat to representative ways, however, overlook the real and limited nature of the document. They also tend to discount the panoply of external and internal constraints that generally have kept the judiciary safe for democracy.

Instead of being detached from the representative process, the judicial system is a direct product of it. Although the Court functions independently, its composition is exclusively the product of executive and legislative discretion. Judges and justices are nominated by the president[52] and appointed with the advice and consent of the senate.[53] Judicial philosophy and decisions respectively do not operate and emanate from a politically sterile environment. Nor are the consequences of judicial review necessarily beyond the influence of the elected branches of government. To the contrary, the judicial appointment process has proved to be a particularly effective means of steering the institution on a course consonant with general or sometimes even specific expectations of the executive and legislative branches. Presidents Washington and Adams, for instance, loaded the Court with firm advocates of a strong central government.[54]

The Court, led by Chief Justice Marshall for the first third of the Nineteenth Century, responded to original executive and legislation expectations and largely helped put into place Federalist political and economic visions.[55] Even a relatively weak chief executive such as Grant used his appointive power effectively to secure political aims and thereby enable Congress to issue paper money.[56] Presidents Harrison, Cleveland and Taft, as noted in the preceding chapter, appointed justices who ushered in and perpetuated the era of Lochnerism.[57] Reacting to the Court's unvarying emphasis upon economic rights, President Roosevelt packed the Court with appointees who would be sympathetic toward his New Deal policies.[58] President Nixon's selection of "law and order" justices,[59] who subsequently helped narrow rights of the accused, and President Reagan's focus upon "family values"[60] are recent examples of how the judiciary may be meaningfully influenced by popular instinct and political input.

Results may not be guaranteed in all specific instances nor, consistent with separation of powers principles, should they be. The power to screen, select and confirm those who will discern the values and fashion the principles to be associated with the constitution, however, has demonstrably profound implications. So potent is the power of appointment that not just the judiciary but representative government itself is responsible for the virtues of Marshall's Federalism and the vices of Lochnerism.

The responsibility of elected institutions for the quality of judicial review is not diminished, even if jurists may become increasingly independent over the course of time. Jurisprudential surprise tends to be more the exception than the norm, at least insofar as conscious expectations of specific performance did not exist at the time of appointment. Purportedly unexpected renderings may be as much attributable to nonideological priorities and interests of the president or Senate as any twists and deviations of the appointee. President Eisenhower's characterization of Chief Justice Earl Warren's appointment as his "biggest mistake,"[61] for instance, did not truly recount a case of betrayal. Eisenhower's selection of Warren constituted a reward for critical assistance received in securing the 1952 Republican presidential nomination.[62] It also was a tactical move calculated to defuse strife between the Nixon and Warren factions of the California Republican Party.[63]

To the extent Warren may have deviated from any presidential expectations, they were unarticulated ones and, if contemplated at all, secondary to more pressing political concerns. Any worry that judges may stray too far from the expectations of those who appoint them can be alleviated by insistence upon more information during the screening process. Although it would contravene separation of power's principles to predetermine a judge's future decision, detailed inquiry into a nominee's assessment of past cases is permissible. Such an examination, although not routinely performed, may demand identification of the values that would inspire a candidate's enunciation of constitutional principle. Evasiveness or reluctance to provide such information might be grounds for denying confirmation. Failure to call for it, however, undercuts any future complaint over judicial performance.

Chief Justice Rehnquist has advanced the notion that jurists, once appointed, are subject to centrifugal forces that invariably move them toward independence and presumably unexpected ways.[64] If that were necessarily so, the democratic force exerted through the appointment power might be depletionary in nature. Rehnquist's own performance, which remains largely coextensive with President Nixon's political agenda, makes him probably the worst exponent of the argument.

Nixon's 1968 campaign included, among other things, assurances that he would appoint to the Court "strict constructionists" committed to law and order and, to curtail the reach of desegregation, a narrow reading of the equal protection clause.[65] Consistent with those aims, Rehnquist regularly has sustained the values which accounted for his appointment. As noted previously, he consistently has opposed actuation of Fourteenth Amendment liberty,[66] resisted expansion of the equal protection clause beyond matters of race[67] and refused a reading of it friendly toward color-conscious remediation.[68] Rehnquist was a swing vote for the effective elimination of busing as a desegregation tool in metropolitan areas.[69] He personally authored the opinion which made the duty to desegregate schools a generally terminal rather enduring obligation[70] and marked the final devolution of the *Brown* mandate. Abiding commitment to the law and order concerns that made him attractive to Nixon continues to be evidenced by Rehnquist's persistent reasoning that has helped narrow the circumstances necessitating *Miranda* warnings,[71] limit the force and reach of the exclusionary rule,[72] uphold pretrial detention[73] and facilitate and expedite capital punishment.[74]

Such performance does not denote a function that is immune to political influence. Nor, given the successes of previous administrations in influencing the Court's direction, is it exceptional. Rehnquist is a product of political forces akin to those responsible for Chief Justice Marshall, who was expected to be and proved to be a reliable champion of Federalist priorities.

The degree to which executive and legislative influence is exerted upon the judiciary, by means of the appointment process, varies. At times, the Senate in particular has evinced a relatively passive and disinterested demeanor toward its confirmation responsibilities.[75] Failure to exercise power, however, should not be confused with an absence of power. When used to its fullest potential, the confirmation process affords the opportunity to investigate a nominee thoroughly and discern his or her acceptability to representative institutions. The Senate's rejection of Judge Robert Bork exemplifies how elected representatives can deny accreditation to candidates whose values are considered worrisome.[76]

In a like event in 1930, the Senate refused to confirm the nomination of Judge John Parker to the Supreme Court. Parker's racist and antilabor sentiments suggested to critics an inability to "discard, if necessary the old precedents of barbaric days, and construe, the constitution and the laws in the light of a modern day, a present civilization."[77] Such observations and the Senate's response to them proved prescient. A quarter of a century later, Parker, after authoring one of the decisions reversed in *Brown v. Board of Education*,[78] emerged as a leader of the renegade Southern judges whose rulings obstructed the desegregation mandate.[79]

The Parker episode illustrates further that the exercise of legislative power is a significant albeit often unappreciated and underused force for influencing the judiciary's works. Whether used forcefully or not, the nomination and confirmation process betokens executive and legislative acquiescence to resultant constitutional judgment. Submission to judicial review is implicit so long as the principle, which relates back to *Marbury v. Madison* and makes the judiciary uniquely responsible for determining constitutional meaning, remains largely unchallenged. Appointment anticipates fulfillment of official responsibilities, which include the ultimate function of constitutional declamation. It accordingly represents consent of those who govern and, in a representative system, consent of the governed to ensuing judicial emanations.

Prudent exercise of appointment powers and even conscientious use of judicial authority do not afford a guarantee against improvident review. Even then, poor judgment should be no more of a basis for disabling the judiciary than it would be for crippling the executive or legislative branches. Faulty or mistaken exercises of power by the elected branches of government, at least in theory, may be more readily redressed by voters. Because the modern system of campaign financing and privileges of incumbency give many representatives the functional equivalent of lifetime tenure, such distinctions may be more illusory than real.

Public tolerance of countless foreign and domestic policy miscalculations, moreover, suggest that good faith performance of duty rather than perfect execution is the citizenry's primary demand. Indulgence of error or wrongdoing is also evident in the interbranch relationships between the legislature and executive, as the relatively gentle congressional inquiry into presidential illegalities concerning funding of Nicaraguan rebels recently has demonstrated.[80] Deference of that order may be explainable on theoretical grounds that voters can expel an elected official whose deeds they disapprove. When examined more carefully, however, such a premise suggests an inverted logic if those more directly franchised by the public trust are freer to abuse it.

Legislative and public control over the judiciary, contrary to myth, does not dissipate once appointive powers are exercised. The judiciary if it ignores dominant values too regularly is vulnerable to redefinition and diminution of its authority. President Roosevelt's court-packing plan, although not implemented, demonstrated how representative forces of government possess ultimate power for societal direction. Nor are checking influences limited to the extreme but little employed recourses of impeachment, judicial restructuring and constitutional amendment. Such drastic options may be proposed but only infrequently are actuated.[81] They seldom are resorted to because judicial declarations generally have proved to be a starting rather then ending point for political intercourse among the Court, legislature and citizenry that ultimately shapes principle satisfactorily to popular taste. Decisions of such magnitude and influence as *Brown v. Board of Education*, even if they run against a strong current of public sentiment, may prove to be acceptable in part because they are so infrequent and eventually so responsive to majoritarian sentiment.

Radical restructuring of society is not a common enterprise of the judiciary. More typical is a refusal to expand privacy rights to include homosexuality or even recognize education as a constitutional interest. The fact that the Court has devoted more time and effort to defending the status quo of slavery and segregation than advancing racial equality denotes how oriented the judiciary has been toward rather than against dominant and established conventions.

The judiciary is not the only branch of government obligated to read the constitution[82] or capable of self-serving interpretation.[83] Nor is it unique in having the potential to disrupt democratic expectations and distort principles. Experience has demonstrated that more profound risks to democratic interests have originated with executive or legislative renditions of the constitution and consequent actions that traumatized important values. Executive or legislative judgment is originally responsible for, among other things, slavery and segregation, forced sterilization, abusive police practices and the suppression of expressive freedoms essential to a democratic society. Insofar as the judiciary has countenanced such policies and practices, the case for judicial review referenced to competing values is enhanced rather than diminished.

Public policy regardless of its source ultimately is susceptible to evaluation by the public. Original pronouncements of constitutional law are constantly subject to revision, as the expansions and contractions of privacy, rights of the accused, expressive freedom and due process and equal protection guarantees show. The past directions of Lochnerism and desegregation and future course of privacy rights and affirmative action may reflect disparate focuses and priorities, but each may be held up as evidence of how the judiciary is subject to the tug of popular will.

Because it has no power to effect compliance absent cooperation of other branches of government and the public, references to the Court as an essentially moral force are not overworked. The legislature can and sometimes does challenge judicial wisdom with subsequent enactments testing the basis, extent and even validity of doctrine. Persistency and pervasiveness of response afford an important indicator of whether values have been misread and rights misconceived. Representative government during the *Lochner* era continued to create laws disputing the Court's calculus and, in the end, it was liberty of contract and a cramped reading of the commerce power that gave way. Likewise, the right to elect an abortion and affirmative action remain subject to the conscious workings of public dissent, legislative challenge and redundant review that will determine their ultimate contours.

In addition to the general political and social forces which effectively yoke the judiciary to the harness of democratic consent, operational constraints further delimit the exercise of power. The Court's control over its agenda tends to be more reactive than initiative. It generally determines neither the nature nor the order in which issues arise. Although the Court is able to send signals regarding its reaction to an issue, such communication is futile without a responsive audience and a principle capable of commanding significant support.

Due to limitations of time and resources, the Court is almost bound to be more passive than active. Of the many constitutional controversies presented to it annually, the Court has the capacity to review relatively few.[84] Even during the *Lochner* era, it scrutinized only a fraction of the regulations that might have been found objectionable.[85] Actual selection of cases to be decided may have a profound impact, but the overall breadth of effect is diminished by the granting of certiorari collectively rather than individually. The Rule of Four, necessitating agreement by four justices for a case to be heard,[86] is augmented by the Rule of Five, requiring five votes for an opinion to have the force of law. The need to secure a majority militates also toward a dedicated search for common ground. Jurisprudential adventurism is more likely to beget a concurring or dissenting opinion that may have future utility but more likely will have no substantive value.

A probably significant but not precisely measurable influence upon judicial performance is the call of history. Jurists have a personal stake in securing a favorable remembrance. Such an interest may promote accountability to multiple generations and thus to the present and future. Reputational concern, however, does not absolutely ensure enlightened decision-making. The political and social forces present in the South when the desegregation mandate was issued, for instance, prompted many local jurists to frame their legacy in terms of what they regarded as a last stand for an unconstitutional way of life. Such motives and designs aside, personal interest in being favorably regarded by history should afford some incentive at least not to repeat past mistakes. That concern is evidenced in the frequent negative references to Lochnerism that still permeate modern jurisprudence.[87] An eye toward other lessons of history, however, should discern that failure to import values can facilitate an equally if not more unflattering legacy.

The ultimate safeguard against abuse of power is not reducible to a tidy formula or singular theory. As an executor of constitutional law, Justice Harlan was chary in his exercise of judicial authority. Contemporary critics of expansive due process review have observed that "No one proceeded with more caution than he did when the validity of . . . legislation was challenged in the name of the Due Process Clause."[88] In helping to construct the right of privacy candidly from value rather than claims of documentary text or design, however, Harlan did not shrink from vitalizing the concept of liberty. Nor did he hide behind analytical frameworks that superficially might appear less value-based. Although recognizing that concepts such as due process and equal protection lend themselves "to 'personal' interpretations by judges," Harlan also realized that formal notions of judicial restraint tended to be "more hollow than real."[89] For Harlan, effectuation of constitutional interests and security for democratic concerns could be achieved:

> only by continued insistence upon respect for the teachings of history, solid recognition of the basic values that underlie our society, and wise application of the great roles that the doctrines of federalism and separation of powers have played [in] preserving American freedoms. Adherence to these principles will not, of course, obviate all constitutional differences of opinion among judges, nor should it. Their continued recognition will, however, go

farther toward keeping most judges from roaming at large in the constitutional field than will the interpolation into the constitution of an artificial and largely illusory restriction on the content of the Due Process Clause.[90]

Harlan's observations do not convert readily into neat or particularly useful campaign rhetoric, or provide fodder for process-oriented theories of restraint, but they are ultimately more trenchant. Informed, enlightened and sensitive performance is an ideal against which all government and not just the judiciary may be measured, although it probably is more easily articulated as a standard than applied. Perfection, in any event, is not the hallmark of a democratic system, which is characterized instead by shared opportunity to influence the course of governance. Given the (1) tasks of self-government that the constitution assigns, (2) varying problems confronting successive generations, (3) availability of checking influences that are effective even if often underestimated, and (4) oppressive consequences when judicial intervention was most needed but not forthcoming, the risks of assuming too much responsibility for vitalizing the constitution seem preferable to those of assuming too little.

Chief Justice Taft observed that "Nothing tends to render judges more careful in their decisions and anxiously solicitous to do exact justice than the consciousness that every act of theirs is to be subject to the intelligent scrutiny of their fellow men, and to their candid criticism."[91] The power to declare "the supreme law of the land," at first blush, may have unsettling implications for a society committed to representative government. Enunciation of constitutional doctrine guided by externally-focused value inquiry, especially to the extent it considers the citizenry's traditions, conscience and expectations, is a process that honors rather than demeans principles of democratic consent. Activism that imports values and processes them into principles that are then affixed to the constitution is an imperative rather than a categorical transgression. Because history evidences that even serious perversions tend to be self-correcting, any interest in optimizing accountability and enhancing democratic linkage should focus upon maximizing the potential for "intelligent scrutiny" of judicial performance.

Pursuant to constitutional dictate, the president is obligated periodically to give "Congress Information of the State of the Union."[92] Political practice has combined with constitutional prescription to beget an annual State of the Union address in which the chief executive communicates his perceptions of material affairs of the nation. Although a like duty is not legally imposed upon the judiciary by the constitution, an analogous public presentation would be a healthy practice. A regular commentary on the state of the institution and constitution could contribute significantly to governmental and public understanding of the nature of and processes responsible for fundamental law. Such awareness might be enhanced further insofar as the Court, like other institutions of government, subjected itself regularly to news conferences, interviews and other forms of public inquiry. Multiplication of opportunities for appraisal would invite scrutiny that was more intelligent and criticism that was more informed and contribute toward an institution more visibly accountable to the citizenry.

Commitment to self-government favors procedures which narrow the distance between the instrumentalities and beneficiaries of governance. Modern technology affords means for heightening the judiciary's and public's respective consciousness of and responsiveness to one another. So far, however, the opportunities for enhancing democratic accountability have not been fully seized. Two decades ago, the notion of cameras in the courtroom was perceived to pose "such a probability [of] prejudice . . . that [they were] deemed inherently lacking in due process."[93] Original resistance to televised court proceedings reflected concern with the impact of the electronic media's presence upon jurors, judges, witnesses and attorneys.[94] Worries that broadcasting may be too intrusive and distracting since have been defused by the state of the art. Such concern is particularly irrelevant in appellate proceedings, where jurors and witnesses are not even present. The possibility that judges or lawyers may be tempted to play to cameras rather than attend to their primary duties is governable by disciplinary rules. Even the Court has reformulated its original position to the extent it now acknowledges that the risk of prejudice does not justify a constitutional ban on all broadcast coverage.[95]

A determination that constitution principle does not prohibit broadcasting of judicial proceedings, however, has not yet translated into affirmative steps to modify institutional bars against electronic coverage. Reluctance to open courtrooms to broadcasting possibly reflects a sense that the judiciary's power as a moral force would be compromised if the public were to see judges as ordinary men and women. If the arguments against televising congressional proceedings afford any insight into the Court's reluctance to allow cameras in the courtroom, it may be that the primary cause of resistance is ego and image. Grounds for opposing coverage of the House and Senate largely narrowed down to worries that members might be identified in embarrassing or unflattering postures when caught off guard. To overcome that concern, rules for coverage restrict camera angles and ambit.

If like anxiety accounts for abiding rules against electronic coverage of judicial proceedings, constitutional and democratic interests suffer congruently. The Court itself has noted that First Amendment protections "share a common core purpose of assuring freedom of communication in matters relating to the functioning of government"[96] and that debate on public issues should be "uninhibited, robust, and wide-open."[97] It is difficult to imagine a governmental function more significant than the judicial process or issues more pertinent than constitutional law. A more hospitable demeanor toward First Amendment values instead of wholesale restrictions upon accessibility would represent a genuine advancement of democratic accountability.

Jefferson's reference to the constitution's architects as "demi-Gods" despite their worldly origins set a tone that continues to enshroud the document and the institution responsible for actuating it in an unfortunate mystique. Intimations that the charter is divinely inspired and that judges interpret it in response to constitutional voices elevate both to unrealistic heights. An activist judiciary may be a conservative one, in a particularly meaningful sense, if it ensures fidelity to important ideals which the constitution itself may not connote but which nonetheless animate principles of a constitutional order. Discernment of values and setting of priorities may engender sharp disagreement, but the Court's actions do not merit a reflexive response that would neutralize the judiciary's essential function and diminish the constitution's significance.

# References

1. *See FCC v. Pacifica Foundation*, 438 U.S. 726, 750-51 (1978).
2. *See Lynch v. Donnelly*, 465 U.S. 668 (1984).
3. *See Memphis v. Greene*, 451 U.S. 100 (1981).
4. *FCC v. Pacifica Foundation*, 438 U.S. at 775-76 (Brennan, J., dissenting).
5. *See Kelley v. Johnson*, 425 U.S. 238 (1976); *Belle Torre v. Boraas*, 416 U.S. 1 (1974).
6. *See Bowers v. Hardwick*, 478 U.S. 186 (1986).
7. *Brown v. Board of Education* 347 U.S. 483, 493 (1954).
8. *Bolling v. Sharpe*, 347 U.S. 487, 499-500 (1954).
9. *San Antonio Independent School District v. Rodriguez*, 411 U.S. 1, 28 (1973).
10. *Moore v. City of East Cleveland*, 431 U.S. at 502.
11. *Id.*
12. *E.g., Roe v. Wade*, 410 U.S. 113, at 152 (1973).
13. *Moore v. City of East Cleveland*, 431 U.S. at 549 (White, J., dissenting).
14. *See id.* at 501.
15. 410 U.S. 113
16. *Id.* at 163.
17. *Id.*
18. *Id.* at 163-64.
19. *Id.* at 174 (Rehnquist, J., dissenting).
20. *See Pro-Choice: A Sleeping Giant Awakes*, NEWSWEEK (April 24, 1989), at 39.
21. *See id.*
22. Ely, *The Wages of Crying Wolf: A Comment on Roe v. Wade*, 82 YALE L.J. 920, 942 (1973).
23. *Id.*
24. *See Moore v. City of East Cleveland*, 431 U.S. at 501.
25. *See Harris v. McRae*, 448 U.S. 297 (1980); *Maher v. Roe*, 432 U.S. 464 (1977).
26. *See H.L. v. Matheson*, 450 U.S. 398 (1981).
27. *See Webster v. Reproductive Health Services*, 109 S.Ct. 3040, 3052 (1989).
28. *Roe v. Wade*, 410 U.S. 113, 174 (1973) (Rehnquist, J., dissenting)
29. *See e.g., Zablocki v. Redhail*, 434 U.S. 374, 407 (1978) (Rehnquist, J., dissenting) (marriage); *Moore v. City of East Cleveland*, 431 U.S. 494, 537 (1977) (Stewart, J. and Rehnquist, J., dissenting) (family); *Vlandis v. Kline*, 412 U.S. 441, 467-68 (1973) (Rehnquist, J., dissenting) (travel).

30. *See* R. JACKSON, THE SUPREME COURT IN THE AMERICAN SYSTEM OF GOVERNMENT 80 (1955).
31. *Wygant v. Jackson Board of Education*, 476 U.S. 267, 273 (1986).
32. *See Regents of the University of California v. Bakke*, 438 U.S. 265, 407 (1978) (Blackmun, J., concurring).
33. *See Pasadena City Board of Education v. Spangler*, 427 U.S. 424 (1976); *Columbus Board of Education v. Penick*, 443 U.S. 449 (1979) (Rehnquist, J., dissenting).
34. *See Craig v. Boren*, 429 U.S. 190, 221-28 (1976) (Rehnquist, J., dissenting).
35. *See* Slaughter-House Cases, 83 U.S. (16 Wall.) 36, 73 (1873).
36. *Id.*
37. U.S. CONST., amend. I.
38. *See, e.g., Central Hudson Gas & Electric Corporation v. Public Service Commission*, 447 U.S. 557, 561-63 (1980); *First National Bank of Boston v. Bellotti*, 435 U.S. 765, 776-77 (1978).
39. *See* 447 U.S. at 595-99 (Rehnquist, J., dissenting).
40. *See* A. MEIKLEJOHN, FREE SPEECH AND ITS RELATIONSHIP TO SELF-GOVERNMENT, 18-19, 22-27 (1948).
41. *See* M. REDISH, FREEDOM OF EXPRESSION 21-22 (1984); T. EMERSON, THE SYSTEM OF FREEDOM OF EXPRESSION 6-7 (1970).
42. *Schaumburg v. Citizens for a Better Environment*, 444 U.S. 620, 644 (1980) (Rehnquist, J., dissenting).
43. *Griswold v. Connecticut*, 381 U.S. 505, 479, (1965) (Black, J., dissenting).
44. *See NAACP v. Alabama*, 357 U.S. 449, 460-61 (1958).
45. *Griswold v. Connecticut*, 381 U.S. at 507 (Black, J., dissenting).
46. *See* D. LLOYD, THE IDEA OF LAW 74-75 (1983).
47. *See* G. GUNTHER, CONSTITUTIONAL LAW 15 (1985).
48. *See* A. HAMILTON, FEDERALIST NO. 78.
49. *See supra* Chapters One, Three and Four.
50. *See* H. MCCLINTOCK, PRINCIPLES OF EQUITY 1-12 (1948).
51. *See id.*
52. U.S. CONST. art. II, §2, cl,2.
53. *Id.*
54. *See* H. ABRAHAM, JUSTICES AND PRESIDENTS 69 (1974).
55. *See id.* at 72-76.
56. *See* L. PFEFFER, THIS HONORABLE COURT 182-85 (1965).
57. *See* H. ABRAHAM, *supra* note 54, at 136-44; A.T. MASON, WILLIAM HOWARD TAFT-CHIEF JUSTICE, 157-58 (1983); THE SUPREME COURT FROM TAFT TO WARREN 67 (1958).
58. *See* J.NOWAK, R.ROTUNDA, J. YOUNG, CONSTITUTIONAL LAW, §4.7, at 147-48 (1986).
59. *See* H. ABRAHAM, *supra* note 54, at 4, 12.
60. *See* Brownstein, *With or Without Supreme Court Charges, Reagan Will Reshape the Federal Bench*, 49 NAT'L. J. 2338, 2340 (1984).
61. R. HODDER-WILLIAMS, THE POLITICS OF THE SUPREME COURT 30 (1980).

62. *See* B. SCHWARTZ, SUPER CHIEF 21–22 (1983); G. WHITE, EARL WARREN: A POLITICAL LIFE 139–44 (1983).
63. *See id.*
64. Rehnquist, Presidential Appointments to the Supreme Court, 2 CONST. COMMENTARY 319, 328–29 (1985).
65. *See* H. ABRAHAM, *supra* note 54, at 4, 12; B. WOODWARD & S. ARMSTRONG, THE BRETHREN 159–61 (1979).
66. *See, e.g., Zablocki v. Redhail*, 434 U.S. 374, 407 (1978) (Rehnquist, J., dissenting); *Vlandis v. Kline*, 421 U.S. 441, 467–68 (1973) (Rehnquist, J., dissenting).
67. *See supra* note 33.
68. *See City of Richmond v. J.A. Croson Company*, 109 S.Ct. 706 (1989); *Wygant v. Jackson Board of Education*, 476 U.S. 267 (1986).
69. *See Milliken v. Bradley*, 418 U.S. 717 (1974).
70. *See Pasadena City Board of Education v. Spangler*, 427 U.S. 424, 437 (1976).
71. *See, e.g., Rhode Island v. Innis*, 446 U.S. 291 (1980).
72. *See, e.g., United States v. Leon*, 104 S.Ct. 3405 (1984).
73. *See, e.g., Bell v. Wolfish*, 441 U.S. 520 (1979).
74. *See, e.g., McCleskey v. Kemp*, 107 S.Ct. 1756 (1987).
75. Typical of such deferential review is a focus merely upon a nominee's "training, experience and judicial temperament." Grossman & Wasby, *The Senate and Supreme Court Nominations: Some Reflections*, 1972 DUKE L.J. 557, 559.
76. *See Privacy and the Undressed*, Newsweek, Oct. 19, 1987, at 100.
77. 72 Cong. Rec. 8,192 (1930) (Sen. Norris).
78. 347 U.S. 483 (1954).
79. *See United States v. Jefferson County Board of Education*, 372 F.2d 836, 863 (5th Cir. 1966) (criticizing Parker's obstructionism on grounds it encouraged school officials not to face up to desegregation duties).
80. *See Reagan's Role at Ollie's Trial*, NEWSWEEK, April 10, 1989, at 29.
81. Despite controversies over busing, school prayer and abortion decisions, Congress has rejected proposals to curb the Court's jurisdiction or amend the constitution. G. GUNTHER, CONSTITUTIONAL LAW 44–48 (1985).
82. All governmental branches are obligated to conform to constitutional standards. *See, e.g., Cooper v. Aaron*, 358 U.S. 1, 18 (1958).
83. The executive branch, for instance, has claimed power to suppress information it unilaterally determines is in the interest of national security and the right to maintain absolute secrecy of presidential communications. The Court, in both instances, rejected the executive's constitutional readings. *See United States v. Nixon*, 403 U.S. 683, 703 (1974) (privilege claim); *New York Times Company v. United States*, 403 U.S. 713, 723 (1971) (national security claim).
84. *See* G. GUNTHER CONSTITUTIONAL LAW 453–54.
85. *See* Vinson, Work of the Federal Courts, 69 S.Ct. V, VI (1949).
86. "Under the well-settled 'rule of four,' certiorari is granted wherever four justices vote a grant...." C. WRIGHT, FEDERAL COURTS 551 (1976).
87. "Rejection of the Lochner heritage is a common starting point for modern Justices: reaction against the excessive intervention of the 'Old Men' of the pre–1937

Judicial Review

Court strongly influenced the judicial philosophies of their successors." G. GUN-
THER, CONSTITUTIONAL LAW 454.

88. *Moore v. City of East Cleveland*, 431 U.S. at 544 (White, J., dissenting).
89. *Griswold v. Connecticut*, 381 U.S. at 501 (Harlan, J., concurring).
90. *Id.* at 501–02 (Harlan, J., concurring).
91. *See* Fein, *Error in the Court*, 75 A.B.A. J. 56, 59 (April 1989)
92. U.S. CONST., art. II, § 3.
93. *Estes v. Texas*, 381 U.S. 532, 542–43 (1965).
94. *Id.* at 544–50.
95. *Chandler v. Florida*, 449 U.S. 560, 574–75, 581 (1981).
96. *Richmond Newspapers, Inc. v. Virginia*, 448 U.S. 555, 575 (1980).
97. *New York Times v. Sullivan*, 376 U.S. 254, 270 (1964).

# Index

# Index

# Index

Roberts, Owen 54
*Roe v. Wade* 23n, 98n, 121–22nn, 128–30, 147n
Roosevelt, Franklin 9, 69, 111–13, 116, 120, 125, 136, 140

Scalia, Antonin 51–52
*Scott v. Sanford* 18–19, 24–25nn, 50, 70n, 116
Segregation 3–4, 8, 15, 17, 57, 66–68, 75, 84–87, 92–94, 108, 118, 128, 134–35, 141–44
*Skinner v. Oklahoma* 73n, 98n
Slaughterhouse cases 23n, 72n, 99n, 148n
Slavery 13–14, 18–19, 27, 33–34, 40, 49–50, 66, 115, 128, 134–35, 141
Sterilization forced 16, 141
Stewart, Potter 147n
Story, Joseph 53
Strict constructionism *see* Theories of review—Literalism

Taft, William 144
Taney, Roger 18–19

Televised court proceedings 145–46
Theories of review: Generally 2, 30, 53–70, 130; Literalism (strict constructionism) 2, 14, 16, 20, 28, 30, 53–56, 130, 138; Neutral principles 2, 53, 59–61; Originalism (framers' intent) 2, 28–29, 53, 56–59; Value referenced jurisprudence 2–3, 15–16, 20–21, 27–28, 32–34, 39, 42, 45, 52–53, 55, 62–65, 75–77, 79, 81, 84, 88, 126–27, 130–36, 141–44

*United States v. Nixon* 24n, 48n, 149n

Wallace, George 91, 96
Warren, Earl 3, 9, 12, 137
Washington, George 17, 136, 140
Watergate 17, 40
*Webster v. Reproductive Health Services* 120n, 147n
White, Byron 101n, 120n, 147n, 149n